Australian Edition

English Grammar Essentials

FOR

DUMMIES

A Wiley Brand

by Wendy M Anderson
Geraldine Woods
Lesley J Ward

WILEY

English Grammar Essentials For Dummies®

Australian edition published by
Wiley Publishing Australia Pty Ltd
42 McDougall Street
Milton, Qld 4064
www.dummies.com

Copyright © 2013 Wiley Publishing Australia Pty Ltd

The moral rights of the authors have been asserted.

National Library of Australia Cataloguing-in-Publication data:

Author:	Anderson, Wendy M
Title:	English Grammar Essentials For Dummies/Wendy M Anderson; Geraldine Woods; Lesley J Ward.
Edition:	Australian ed.
ISBN:	9781118493311 (pbk.)
Series:	For Dummies
Notes:	Includes index
Subjects:	English language — Grammar.
	English language — Grammar — Problems, exercises, etc.
	English language — Self-instruction.
Other Authors/ Contributors:	Woods, Geraldine
	Ward, Lesley J
Dewey Number:	428.2

Cover image: © Tim Hester / Alamy

Typeset by diacriTech, Chennai, India

Printed in Singapore by C.O.S Printers Pte Ltd

10 9 8 7 6 5 4 3 2 1

About the Authors

Wendy M Anderson spent the first decade or so of her professional life as an English teacher before reinventing herself as an education publisher. She then moved on to teaching editing and professional writing to adult learners, guest lecturing in grammar and tutoring in a university English department, and facilitating corporate workshops in business communication. She occupies the remaining daylight hours (and lots of the non-daylight hours too) enjoying the feast or famine world of the freelance writer/editor and has been widely published. She lives on the Bass Coast and strongly denies all accusations that she has a few wallabies loose in the top paddock.

Geraldine Woods career as a grammarian began in her elementary school, which in those days was called 'grammar school' for very good reason. With the guidance of a series of nuns carrying long rulers, she learned how to diagram every conceivable type of sentence. She has been an English teacher for over 25 years and has written 40 books, give or take a few. She loves baseball, Chinese food and the novels of Jane Austen.

Lesley J Ward has worked in the publishing industry for over 30 years, editing and proofreading. She is a founder member of the UK Society of Editors and Proofreaders (SfEP), and regularly leads training courses for SfEP, the Irish Book Publishers' Association and the London College of Communications. She is also a distance-learning tutor for the Publishing Training Centre. She lives in Berkshire and is notorious for being a harmless eccentric/dangerous radical who refuses to have email.

Publisher's Acknowledgements

We're proud of this book; please send us your comments through our online registration form located at http://dummies.custhelp.com.

Some of the people who helped bring this book to market include the following:

Acquisitions, Editorial and Media Development

Acquisitions Editor: Clare Dowdell

Editorial Manager: Dani Karvess

Production

Cartoon: Glenn Lumsden

Proofreader: Charlotte Duff

Technical Reviewer: Margaret McKenzie

Indexer: Don Jordan, Antipodes Indexing

Every effort has been made to trace the ownership of copyright material. Information that enables the publisher to rectify any error or omission in subsequent editions is welcome. In such cases, please contact the Legal Services Section of John Wiley & Sons Australia, Ltd.

Contents at a Glance

Table of Contents

Introduction

* *

Chances are you're reading this book because you're not confident about what constitutes 'proper grammar'. Perhaps you went to school in an era when teachers didn't believe in worrying kids about pedantic things like correct spelling and complete sentences. Or, maybe you did study grammar but you found it boring, switched off and have forgotten most of the rules. Now, you may feel that your language skills aren't as good as they need to be. Feeling that you are being judged on your communication can be stressful and make you feel self-conscious. And it's worse if everyone else seems to understand, or if you find to your horror that the boss or tutor is one of those people who even uses perfect grammar in text messages.

English grammar is not that scary. You don't have to memorise all of the technical terms and, once you get started, you'll find that most of it is pretty logical. In this book we present you with strategies and tips that help you make the right decision when you're tossing up whether to use *who* or *whom*, or trying to remember if you should put the apostrophe in *its*. We explain *what* you're supposed to do when, tell you *why* a particular way of doing things is correct or incorrect, and even show you *how* to revise your sentences if your grammar checker puts a squiggly green line under some part of your sentence. Once you understand the reason for a particular grammar choice, you'll pick the correct option automatically.

About This Book

In this book, we concentrate on common errors and tell you what's what in the sentence, in logical, everyday English, not in obscure terminology. When we do use a key term, you'll generally find it in *italics* with a definition or example (or both) close by. You don't have to read the chapters in order, but you can. And you don't have to read the whole book. Just browse through the table of contents and look for things that have always troubled you.

Foolish Assumptions

We assume that you, the reader, already speak English (although you may have learned it as a foreign language) and that you want to speak and write it better. We also assume that you're a busy person with better things to do than worry about what a *relative clause* looks like. You want to speak and write well, but you don't want to get a doctorate in English grammar. (Smart move. Doctorates in English don't move you very far up the salary scale.)

This book is for you if you aspire to

- ✔ achieving better marks for your essays
- ✔ landing a job with better pay or a higher status
- ✔ having your speech and writing present you as an educated, intelligent person
- ✔ being able to write and say exactly what you mean
- ✔ developing a sound understanding of good grammar.

Icons Used in This Book

Throughout this book you can find useful icons to help you note specific types of information. Here's what each icon means:

Have you ever been confused by the message your grammar checker gives you when it puts a wiggly line under a possible problem and asks you to 'consider revising' some part of your sentence? Your days of confusion end here. This little fellow appears at the same points that a wiggly line would appear, and the information alongside it tells you exactly how to revise those troublesome sentences.

Wherever you see this icon, you'll find helpful strategies for understanding the structure of the sentence or for choosing the correct word form.

Not every grammar trick has a built-in trap, but some do. This icon tells you how to avoid common mistakes as you unravel a sentence.

Where to Go from Here

Before you get started, one last word. Actually, two last words. *Trust yourself.* You already know a lot. You'd be amazed how much grammar can be absorbed by osmosis from day-to-day language, even if you don't know the technical terms. So be brave. Dip a toe into the sea of grammar. The water's fine.

'You're charged with illegal use of a verb, omission of an apostrophe and — something the magistrate is unlikely to hand down — an incomplete sentence.'

Chapter 1

Grappling with Grammar

* *

* *

*G*ood communication and good grammar go hand in hand. The very point of using language is to express and exchange ideas in a way that conveys them clearly, with as few misunderstandings as possible. Sure, an occasional 'Oh, you know what I mean' is not going to stop the world from turning or upset your friends and family, but if you need to impress somebody, you need your communication to be accurate. If you want your job application to shine, your presentation to captivate or your documents to be precise, using good grammar will help you to achieve these things.

Of course, you probably already have pretty good grammar. Most people learn the basics of language use as if by osmosis, picking it up without necessarily understanding the rules. After all, you're likely to have been talking almost all of your life and have probably forgotten when and how you first learned to read and write. But the fact that you have this book in your hands means that you have decided that learning *better* grammar is a valuable strategy. Yay you! This book will help you become a better communicator.

In this chapter, we look closely at what constitutes proper grammar and consider what makes Australian English unique. We also take a trip back in time to revisit probably the first thing you were taught about grammar as we consider the very basic unit of communication: the word.

Grasping Grammar: Good and Proper

Rightly or wrongly, your audience or readers judge you by the words you use and the way you string them together. Listen to the speech of the people in movies. An uneducated character sounds different from someone with five diplomas on the wall. The dialogue reflects reality: educated people follow certain rules when they speak and write. In fact, people who use language according to formal grammar rules are said to be speaking *properly*. If you want to present yourself as an educated person, you have to follow those rules too.

Actually, several different types of grammar exist, including *historical* (how language has changed through the centuries) and *comparative* (comparing languages). Vintage grammar-geeks and gurus loved to complicate things. But don't worry; we love to keep things simple. In this book, we use the best bits of the two easiest, most familiar ways of presenting the rules of grammar to come up with what's proper.

Descriptive grammar gives names to things — the parts of speech, or word groups, and parts of a sentence. When you learn descriptive grammar, you understand what every word *is* (its part of speech) and what every word *does* (its function in the sentence). Learning some grammar terms has a couple of important advantages — to be clear about *why* a particular word or phrase is correct or incorrect, and to be able to understand the explanations and advice given by your computer's grammar checker or in a dictionary or style guide.

Functional grammar tells you how words behave when they're doing their jobs properly. It guides you to the right expression — the one that fits what you're trying to say — by ensuring that the sentence is put together correctly. When you're agonising over whether to say *I* or *me*, you're solving a problem of functional grammar. Most of the grammar we use in this book is functional grammar.

So here's the formula for better grammar: a little descriptive grammar plus a lot of functional grammar. Better grammar equals better self-expression. And better self-expression equals improved self-confidence. And with improved self-confidence, anything is possible. The news is all good!

Using Aussie English

In the Middle Ages, *grammar* meant the study of Latin, because Latin was the language of choice for educated people. In fact, knowing Latin grammar was so closely associated with being an educated person that the word *grammar* was also used to refer to any kind of learning. That's why *grammar schools* were called grammar schools; they were places of learning — and not just learning about how Latin and English work.

These days, grammar is the study of language — specifically, how words are put together to create meaning. Through time, grammar has also come to mean a set of standards that you have to follow in order to speak and write correctly. No doubt in your career as a student, you discovered that different teachers have different pet hates — English teachers included. The emphasis placed on the importance of certain points of grammar differs from classroom to classroom. Don't worry; we're consistent.

The accepted way that English is spoken is called *usage*, and this includes both *standard* and *non-standard usage*. Standard usage is the one that is regarded as proper. It consists of the commonly accepted correct patterns of speech and writing that mark an educated person in our society. You can find standard usage in government documents, in formal newspapers and magazines, and in textbooks. Non-standard usage includes slang and just plain bad grammar. It's common in everyday conversations, but should be avoided in formal situations.

Furthermore, the way the rules and patterns of grammar are applied varies in different English-speaking countries. Standard Australian English isn't the same as either standard American English or standard British English. Certainly, we choose different standard spellings for the same word (such as –ise endings in Australia versus –ize endings in America) or different words for the same thing (for example, a sidewalk in America is a pavement in England and a footpath in Australia). More than this, the way we use certain punctuation marks varies, and sometimes we even put words in a different order to express the same meaning.

Examples of non-standard Australian English include using *verse* as a verb meaning 'to compete against' (*Our team is versing yours next week*) and choosing *youse* as a plural form of *you* (*Youse can all come too*). Using non-standard Australian English isn't likely to get you that promotion you wanted. (But using plain English, where you keep your language clear, might — for more on this, see Chapter 10.)

So how do we decide what is standard Australian English? We refer to authorities. We use Australian dictionaries and Australian style guides. We follow the advice provided by the Australian National Dictionary Centre at the Australian National University, and scour the bulletins on English in Australia published by the Department of Linguistics at Macquarie University. Relax. In this book, all the research has been done for you. That's a promise.

Having a Quick Squiz at Aussie Words

Today, just as your average Australian *dunny* is indoors, your average Australian neighbour is not a *bush cocky*. Uniquely Australian language is alive and well and living in the suburbs. (All italicised terms in this section are defined in the list at the end of the section.)

Naturally, the earliest examples of *true blue* Australian language come from the convict days. Early Australian vocabulary was borrowed from various forms of British English. The *crims* sent here by *Her Maj* were not well educated, and spoke a kind of street language that set them apart from the wealthy and privileged. *Lagging* on your *mates* has always been un-Australian, and *dobbing* continues to be a social crime in classrooms today — only *big-noting* or being a *wowser* are worse. Australia's convict heritage has even been blamed for the all-too-prevalent *tall poppy syndrome* that characterises the culture.

Australians took other words that we claim as Australian English from the languages of our indigenous peoples. Let's face it, what would anyone who'd never been *within cooee* of one before call a *wallaby* or a *wobbegong*? And in households all over the nation, high-tech equipment regularly *goes bung*.

Making fun of others and being irreverent has always been a feature of Australian language. *Bananabenders* and *Sandgropers* argue about who has the best beaches. We affectionately refer to each other as *dags* or *ratbags*. Even our first female prime minister is regularly referred to as a *ranga*.

Even our *pollies* themselves help keep Australian English healthy. John Howard gave us *economic rationalism* when he was prime minister. And where else in the world would there be *anti-hoon legislation*?

- ✓ anti-hoon legislation: laws to curb anti-social driving

- ✓ Bananabender: person from Queensland

- ✓ big-noting: bragging about oneself

- ✓ bush cocky: farmer

- ✓ crim: criminal

- ✓ dag: a likeable person who is unconcerned about fashion

- ✓ dinky-di: genuine

- ✓ dobbing: informing on another

- ✓ dunny: toilet

- ✓ economic rationalism: market- and money-oriented economic policy

- ✓ goes bung: breaks down (from the Yagara language, originally meaning dead)

- ✓ Her Maj: Her Majesty the Queen of England

- ✓ lagging: informing on another

- ✓ pollie: politicians

- ✓ ranga: person with red hair

- ✓ ratbag: an amusing troublemaker

- ✓ Sandgroper: person from West Australia

- ✓ squiz: look or glance

- ✓ tall poppy syndrome: the systematic criticism of high achievers

- ✓ true blue: patriotic Australian

- ✓ wallaby: small pouched marsupial like a kangaroo

- ✓ within cooee: in close proximity to

- ✓ wobbegong: A species of shark

- ✓ wowser: Person who tries to impose their own strict moral code on others

Choosing Levels of English

So, using good grammar clearly sounds like a great idea, but you may not always need to use standard English because the language of choice depends on your situation. Here's what we mean. Imagine that you're hungry. How would you invite someone to join you for lunch?

Would you care to accompany me to lunch?

Wanna go grab a bite?

Different levels of English are used in everyday life. We call the first example *formal English*, and the second example *informal English*. If you're like most people, you switch between levels of English dozens of times each day without even thinking about it. You choose the most suitable level of language depending on where you are, what's going on and who your audience is.

Impressing with formal English

Formal English shows that you've trotted out your best behaviour in someone's honour. You may use formal English when you have less power, importance and/or status than the other person in the conversation. You may also use it when you have *more* power, importance or status than the other person (to maintain the distance between you). Think of formal English as English on its best behaviour and wearing a business suit. If you're in a situation where you want to look your best, or in which you're being judged, use formal English.

Situations and types of writing that call for formal English include

- authoritative reference books
- business letters and emails (from individuals to businesses, as well as from or between businesses)
- homework

- ✔ important conversations such as job interviews, university interviews, parole hearings, sessions with teachers in which you explain that it wasn't you who did what they think you did, that sort of thing

- ✔ letters to government officials

- ✔ notes or letters to teachers

- ✔ office memos

- ✔ reports

- ✔ speeches, presentations and formal oral reports.

Chances are formal English is the one that gives you the most trouble. In fact, it's probably why you bought this book. So, the grammar lessons you'll find here deal with how to handle formal English, because that's where the rewards for knowledge are greatest.

Chatting in informal English

Informal English is casual and often strays from the rules, even breaking some. It's the tone of most everyday speech, especially between equals. In informal English we take short cuts and combine words: *let's, we've, I'll*. Using informal English is fine for conversations, emails to friends or a note to your brother, but not for writing an essay or a business report.

In the written form, informal English also relaxes the punctuation rules. Sentences run together, dashes connect all sorts of things, and half-sentences pop up regularly. This book is in conversational English because we like to think we're chatting with you, the reader, not teaching grammar in a classroom. Think of informal English as being like English in jeans and a T-shirt: perfectly comfortable and presentable, but not suitable as corporate attire.

Specifically, informal English is appropriate in these situations:

- ✔ comments made on public internet sites

- ✔ communication (including by email or snail mail) with your extended personal community of family, friends and acquaintances

✔ incidental conversations (but not in writing) with bosses, teachers and work colleagues

✔ fiction and memoir writing.

Labelling Words

No doubt you've been in the frustrating position of having to try to decode what someone is trying to tell you about 'What's-her-name ... You know ... The one who works at that place ... She has a sort of large thingamabob'. Without the right words, the correct labels, you cannot understand the message. The same is true when talking about language or, more specifically, about grammar. You don't need to be a professor or a walking dictionary, but you do need to understand the key terms so that we can communicate efficiently. So we're going to introduce you to (or just reacquaint you with) some of the most important grammar terms, starting with the labels used for *word classes* or *parts of speech*. Understanding these is the first step to better grammar.

Nouns

We use nouns to provide a name or label. We have nouns for people (*lawyer, Vincent*); places (*beach, Monkey Mia*); objects (*pen, bird*); feelings (*happiness, boredom*); concepts (*accountability, freedom*); qualities (*bravery, intelligence*); ideas (*imagination, notion*); and activities (*golf, dancing, shopping*). Nouns are rarely troublemakers, but in Chapter 5 we take a peek at how they work in descriptions, while in Chapter 7 the connection between nouns and capital letters is made clear.

Pronouns

The name *pronoun* makes this part of speech sound either like a highly skilled, professional (pro) noun, or a class of word that is totally in favour of (pro) nouns. While both are possible, neither is entirely correct. A *pronoun* is a word that can be used in the place of a *noun*. (See how handy it is to have basic grammar vocabulary at your fingertips? Some parts of speech are defined according to their relationship to other word classes.) Chapter 4 explains how to peak with pronouns, but, in the meantime, here's an example of how *pronouns* substitute for *nouns* to minimise tedious repetition in communication:

> **With nouns (yawn):** If *Kelly* wants to bring *Kelly's* friend, *Kelly* is welcome to do so.

> **With pronouns:** If Kelly wants to bring *her* friend, *she* is welcome to do so.

> **Also with pronouns:** If *you* want to bring *your* friend, *you* are welcome to do so.

Verbs

If you delve back into the darkest corner of your brain, you can probably dimly recall chanting the definition, 'A verb is a doing word'. Powering your language is exactly what the verb is 'doing'. Verbs refer to actions (*eat, write, take*), conditions (*seem, appear, become*) or states of being (*am, is, are*). They're also the key to understanding when a sentence is grammatically correct, so these guys deserve close attention. To locate a verb in a sentence, you need to ask yourself these questions: *What's happening? What is?* The word that provides the answer is the *verb*.

Because they change their form and attach to other verbs or other parts of speech to change their meaning, verbs can be tricky. But verbs have power, and understanding how they work is probably the most essential of all grammar essentials. Chapter 2 takes you further into the world of verbs.

Adjectives

When we add more information to a *noun* or *pronoun*, the word we use is called an *adjective*. Adjectives add to, describe or modify nouns and pronouns. They can be found lurking either in front of a noun or pronoun, or after a special kind of *verb* called a *linking verb* (you can read all about verbs in Chapter 2). Because adjectives add colour and detail to our language, they're worth careful consideration, so Chapter 5 provides ample advice but, basically, adjectives work like this:

Before a noun: The *sneaky* adjective attaches itself to the *unsuspecting* noun.

Before a pronoun: The noun is the *unsuspecting* one.

After a linking verb: The adjective is *sneaky* and the noun is *unsuspecting*.

Adverbs

Another of those grammar chants you may have learned at one stage goes like this: 'An adverb adds meaning to a verb by telling us how, when, where or why a thing is done'. While that's true, it's only part of the adverb story. Adverbs can also be used to modify adjectives or even other adverbs. Another thing you may vaguely remember is that adverbs often end with –*ly*. True. But not all adverbs end with those letters, and *lovely* is an adjective. So, reading Chapter 5 will help you to master adverbs and to write so that your descriptions say precisely what you mean. Here are some adverbs at work:

With a verb: The sun shines *brightly*.

With an adjective: The day feels *unbearably hot*.

With another adverb: The sea glistens *most enticingly*.

Verbals

What do you get when you cross a verb with a noun, or an adjective, or an adverb? Answer: a *verbal*. A *verbal* is a word that looks like a *verb*, or part of a verb, but is not acting like a verb. It is being used as another *part of speech*. Even its label, *verbal*, suggests that this part of speech must have something to do with verbs. So, you need to know about these two-timers so that you don't confuse them with the real verbs in your writing. Take a look at these examples:

As a noun: *Studying* gives me nightmares.

As an adjective: I rest my *tired* brain.

As an adverb: She should try *to sleep*.

Determiners

There was once a word class for just three words: *a, the, an*. They formed the word group called *articles*. But what makes those three little words so special? Well ... Ummm ... Nothing really. They do the same job as lots of other words. So, contemporary grammar-gurus include articles in a word class called *determiners*. A raft of words that also fit into other classes work extra shifts as determiners. Like articles, determiners go in front of a noun or a group of words that's doing the work of a noun, and tell you how specific or otherwise something is.

Common determiners are words such as *the, both, every, my, his, our, this, that, these, those, each, ten*. As you can no doubt see, some of those words look suspiciously like other parts of speech — pronouns, for example, (*my, his, our*) or adjectives (*each, both, ten*). Different grammar books or teachers may even refer to them as such. What you need to know is that we prefer the simplest, most logical way of explaining language, so throughout this book, we'll stick with the label *determiner*.

Prepositions

If all the parts of speech were to form a sporting team, Preposition would be the easy-going one who fills in wherever and whenever required. During the game, Preposition would consistently pass the ball to Noun or Pronoun so they can score the points. *Prepositions* are unassuming but important contributors to the language game.

Prepositions show a relationship between a noun and another word. We can relate the two nouns *book* and *wombat* by using various prepositions to express different ideas. The book could be *about* the wombat, *beside* the wombat or maybe *behind* the wombat. Which would mean that the wombat was *in* the book, *near* the book and *in front of* the book.

Prepositions (the words in italics) come in front of a noun or group of words acting as a noun. That's why they're called *pre + positions*. In Chapter 8, we see how they work with pronouns, where they sometimes cause problems but, generally, they're helpful little words.

Conjunctions

The fact that the label *conjunction* contains the word *junction* is no coincidence. Just as a junction connects two or more roads, so a *conjunction* connects two or more words. Common joining words are *and, but, because, so, or*. That's pretty straightforward, but conjunctions come in several varieties, which is important to understand when you need to connect whole ideas rather than just individual words. So you can find out about two-part conjunctions in Chapter 8, while Chapter 10 shows you how important they are for connecting ideas in a logical way.

Chapter 2

Controlling Verbs

*E*very sentence needs a *verb*. This group of words refers to actions, conditions or states of being to tell you what's happening in the sentence. And the verb connects with another group of words (called the *subject*) to tell you who performs the action of the verb.

Verbs are at the core of a sentence, and you should start with the verb when you want to do anything to your sentence — including correct it. So, in this chapter we look at different types of verbs, how to find them and how they fit together with subjects.

Verifying Verbs

Verbs come in various shapes and sizes — action and linking, auxiliary and main, regular and irregular, singular and plural. They can be present, past and future. The *tense* of a verb tells you when the action is happening. Making sure that you have the right verb in the right place is the key to understanding sentences. So in this section, we're going to reacquaint ourselves with the different types of verbs, see how they often hang out together in groups, and give you the lowdown on how to locate the verb in a sentence.

Happening with action verbs

Action verbs are the real 'doing words'. Something happens in a sentence with an action verb:

> Lumpy *buys* and then *devours* three pasties as a snack. (*Buys* and *devours* are action verbs.)

> Ed *had answered* the question even before it *was asked*. (*Had answered* and *was asked* are action verbs.)

Don't let the name *action* fool you. Some action verbs aren't particularly energetic: *think, sit, stay, have, sleep, dream* and so on. Besides describing the perfect day off, these words are also action verbs.

Being with linking verbs

Not all verbs are as busy as action verbs. *Linking verbs* are also called *being verbs* because they express states of being — *what is, will be* or *was*. (Not surprisingly, the verb used to express the state of being is often the verb *to be*.) You can think of a linking verb as an equals sign in the middle of your sentence. In the same way that an equals sign tells you that the parts on either side of it are the same value, the word *is* links two ideas and says that those ideas are the same. For example:

> Yasmin *is* a beautiful young woman. (Yasmin = a beautiful young woman; *is* = linking verb.)

> Bobo *will be* angry if you take away her hair straightener. (Bobo = angry; *will be* is a linking verb.)

> Midge *was* the last surfer to leave the water. (Midge = last surfer; *was* is a linking verb.)

Not all linking verbs are forms of the verb *to be*. Other verbs work in the same way — check out these examples:

> With his twinkling eyes and shy smile, Damian *seems* harmless. (Damian = harmless; *seems* is a linking verb.)

> Lucinda's parents *remained* confident. (Lucinda's parents = confident; *remained* is a linking verb.)

Seems and *remained* are expressing states of being, so they're linking verbs too. Any verb that works as an equals sign in the sentence is a linking verb.

Sensory verbs — verbs that express information you receive through the senses of sight, hearing, smell, taste and touch — may also be linking verbs:

> Even after a bath to remove all the jam, Teddy still *feels* sticky. (Teddy = sticky; *feels* is a linking verb.)

> Uri's violin solo *sounds* horrible, like an animal in pain. (Uri's violin solo = horrible; *sounds* is a linking verb.)

Some verbs can act as both linking and action verbs — obviously not at the same time. Verbs, especially those that refer to the five senses, may be linking verbs, but only if they are equating two ideas. In the sentence about Teddy, *feels* is a linking verb. Here's a different sentence with the same verb:

> Yasmin *feels* the silk of Stella's new dress.

In this sentence, *feels* is not a linking verb because you're not saying:

> Yasmin = silk

Instead, you're saying that Yasmin is admiring Stella's dress and can't help touching the material.

Here's a list of the most common linking verbs:

- ✔ forms of *to be*: am, are, is, was, were, will be, shall be, has been, have been, had been, could be, should be, would be, might have been, could have been, should have been, shall have been, will have been, must have been, must be

- ✔ sensory verbs: look, sound, taste, smell, feel

- ✔ words that express shades of meaning in reference to a state of being: appear, grow, remain, seem, stay, turn.

Helping out in verb groups

You've probably noticed that some of the verbs identified throughout this chapter (such as *devours* and *remain*) are single words and others (such as *will answer* and *has made*) are made up of more than one word. The extra words are called *helping verbs* or *auxiliary verbs*. They help the main verb express meaning, usually changing the time, or *tense*, of the action. (For more on tense, see Chapter 8.) These groups of verbs can be called *compound verbs*, but we're going to refer to them by the very user-friendly and logical name *verb groups*.

Here is a sentence with verb groups:

> He *had been singing* karaoke all night, and *should have stopped* after the first song. (In *had been singing*, *singing* is the main verb; *had* and *been* are auxiliary verbs. In the verb group *should have stopped*, *stopped* is the main verb.)

Without auxiliary verbs, we would still understand the general idea of the sentence from the main verb. *He singing karaoke all night* conveys the sense of action and meaning, but it's not a grammatically correct sentence.

 Sometimes, your grammar checker may warn that your sentence contains a 'split verb phrase'. Here's what it's trying to tell you. The parts of the verb group in the sentence have been separated by other words, as in these examples:

> Jules *was* totally *confused* by her reply. (*Was* = auxiliary; *confused* = main verb.)

> Jules *will* also *have* completely *missed* the clues. (*Will* = auxiliary; *have* = auxiliary; *missed* = main verb.)

Rest assured that this is not a mistake. Split verb phrases are a regular feature of our language landscape. The reason you should look again at your sentence and consider revising it is that in formal English the parts of the verb group should be kept together. So the sample sentences become:

> Jules *was confused* totally by her reply.

> Jules also *will have missed* the clues completely.

These formal sentences don't seem to emphasise the same points though, do they? And the meaning of the split verb versions is perfectly clear. So, consider whether or not to revise the sentence according to your audience and why you split the verb in the first place.

Finding the whole verb

When you try to crack a sentence, you should always start by identifying the verb. To find the verb, read the sentence and ask two questions:

- ✔ What's happening?
- ✔ What is? (*or* What word is acting as a giant equals sign?)

If you get an answer to the first question, you have an action verb. If you get an answer to the second question, you have a linking verb. Check the following sentence:

> Archie flew around the room and then swooped into his cage for a birdseed snack.

If you ask 'What's happening?' your answer is *flew* (*Archie . . . flew*) and *swooped* (*Archie . . . swooped*). *Flew* and *swooped* are action verbs.

If you ask 'What is?' you get no answer because no linking verb is in the sentence.

Try another:

> Bill's new tattoo will be larger than his previous nine tattoos.

What's happening? Nothing. You have no action verb. What is? Look for the equals sign:

> Bill's new tattoo = larger

The words that stand for the equals sign are *will be*. So *will be* is a linking verb.

Simplifying Subjects

All complete sentences contain verbs — words that express action or state of being. So, someone or something must also be present in the sentence doing the action or being of that verb. The *who* or *what* you're talking about in relation to the action or state of being expressed by the verb is the *subject*. In this section, we're going to show you how to locate the subject, even if it's hiding out somewhere sneaky.

Locating the subject

The first question to ask about a sentence is *What's the verb?* To find the verb, you need to ask *What's happening?* or *What is?* After you uncover the verb, ask *who* or *what* is doing it. The answer to that question is the subject!

Try one:

> Jonah straightens his hair every day.

1. Ask yourself the question: What's happening?

Answer: *Straightens. Straightens* is the verb.

2. Ask yourself: Who or what *straightens*?

Answer: *Jonah* straightens. *Jonah* is the subject.

A subject is always a *noun* (person, place, thing or idea) or a noun equivalent. A 'someone' is always a person and a 'something' is a thing, place or idea. When the subject is a noun equivalent, it is a *pronoun* (a word such as *he*, *they* or *it* that substitutes for a noun) or a noun group (a group of words doing the work of a noun).

Baring the complete subject

In squillions of sentences, the subject contains more than just one word. For example:

> That huge slice of gooey chocolate mud cake looks delicious.

To identify the subject in this sentence, we first locate the verb (*looks*) and then ask the subject question (*Who* or *what* looks?).

Now, the answer to the subject question for this sentence is a bit tricky. Is it *That huge slice of gooey chocolate mud cake* or is it simply *cake*? Both answers are actually correct.

That huge slice of gooey chocolate mud cake is known as the *complete subject*. The complete subject contains all the words that give information about the person or thing performing the verb. The complete subject is also a *noun group*, a group of words doing the same job as a single-word noun in a sentence.

The single-word subject (in this case *cake*) is known as the *simple subject* or the *bare subject*. It's the complete subject after having been stripped naked. Bare of any and all extra information and decoration, the subject is always simply a noun or a pronoun (which stand in for nouns).

Uncovering a hidden subject

Although the subject usually comes before the verb, not every sentence follows that order. Sometimes (especially if you're having a conversation with Yoda from *Star Wars*) a subject hides at the end of the sentence or in some other weird place. Consider this:

> At the water's edge stood several confused Jedi knights.

The verb in this sentence is *stood* but it's not the water's edge doing the standing, it's the Jedi knights. Here, the subject follows the verb. Tricky, huh?

If you ask yourself who or what is performing the verb, and answer that question according to the meaning of the sentence — not according to the word order — you'll be fine. The key is to put the subject questions (who? what?) in front of the verb. Then think about what the sentence is actually saying. And voila! Your subject will appear.

Commanding an implied subject

Consider the following:

> Be quiet.

> Give me that.

What do these sentences have in common? Yes, they're all bossy comments you've heard all your life. More importantly, they're all commands. The verbs give orders: *be, give*. So where's the subject in these sentences?

Here's what happens:

1. **Ask yourself:** What's happening? What is?

   Answer: *Be, give.*

2. **Ask yourself:** Who *be, give*?

   Answer: Ummmm . . .

The second question appears to have no answer, but you do know who's supposed to be doing these things (or who's not doing them): *You*. They mean *You* be quiet. *You* give me that. Grammarians say that the subject is *implied*. The subject is *you*, even though *you* isn't in the sentence and even though *you* may choose not to hear any of the commands.

Making Subjects and Verbs Agree

Subjects and verbs must form pairs. We grammar-lovers call this process *agreement*. The verb must match up with, or *agree*, with the subject. If you're a native speaker of English, you correctly match subjects and verbs whenever you speak. Your ear for proper language allows you to create these subject–verb pairs without much thought. Helping you is the fact that, in most cases, you use exactly the same form of the verb for both singular and plural verbs. In this section, we focus on how to be a good matchmaker of subject–verb pairs.

 To find the subject–verb pair, first find the verb. Ask yourself the verb question: *What's happening?* or *What is?* The answer is the verb. Then ask the subject question: *Who* or *what is performing the verb?* The answer is the subject.

Separating singles from plurals

English verbs are adjusted a little to match their subject — the person or thing performing the verb. So we say *John leaps* when just one John is doing the leaping (John is *singular*). But we say *the dancers leap* when more than one person is leaping (*dancers* is *plural*). Notice how, in these sample sentences, singular subjects (just one) are matched with singular verbs, and plural subjects (more than one) are matched with plural verbs:

> Gerard the garden gnome loves the fairy. (*Gerard* = singular subject, *loves* = singular verb)

> His kookaburra friends laugh at him. (*friends* = plural subject, *laugh* = plural verb)

Never try to match a singular subject with a plural verb or vice versa. The result is a disastrous mismatch.

 The pronoun *you* can refer to one person (singular) or to a group (plural). This can cause confusion, which is why people sometimes add '... I don't mean "you" personally ...' to make it clear that they didn't mean any insult specifically to the person they were speaking to — they were just generally insulting the whole family or all their work colleagues!

Adjusting verbs to match subjects

In English, the verb shows the time the action or 'being' took place — past, present or future — and whether that action is finished or on-going. We call this *verb tense* and grammar-geeks have lots of special labels to identify all the possible variations. We're not going to bore you with all the details. Quite honestly, you don't even need to know the labels to be able to make subjects and verbs agree, but you'll find them with the examples just in case seeing them helps you to learn (or remember) better grammarspeak.

Remaining regular

Many verbs fit into the category known as *regular verbs*. They don't need much adjusting to match up with subjects. Here are some examples, all with the regular verb *to snore*, of tenses that use the same form for both singular and plural subjects:

> Cassie *snored* constantly, but her cousins *snored* only on long weekends. (The *simple past tense* verb *snored* matches both the singular subject Cassie and the plural subject *cousins*.)

> Peter *will snore* if he eats cheese before bed, but his budgies *will snore* whenever they fall asleep. (The *simple future* tense verb *will snore* matches both the singular subject *Peter* and the plural subject *budgies*.)

Peter *had snored* long before his tonsils were removed, but on sleepovers all his school friends *had snored* too. (The *past perfect* verb *had snored* matches both the singular subject *Peter* and the plural subject *school friends*.)

By the time the movie is over, Peter *will have snored* for at least ten minutes, and his budgies *will have snored* for even longer. (The *future perfect* verb *will have snored* matches both the singular subject *Peter* and the plural subject *budgies*.)

Nearly all regular verbs are the same for both singular and plural. The singular verb ends in *s* and the plural form doesn't. Here are some examples of regular present tense verbs:

Singular	*Plural*
the dog bites	the dogs bite
Lucinda rides	they ride
she screams	the girls scream

Changing irregularly

Unfortunately, communication would be severely limited if you stuck to just the unchanging tenses. Even though irregular verbs (the ones that don't follow a regular pattern) are the minority, they are a pretty important and often powerful little group — *I bring, he (bringed??) brought; he gives, they (gived??) gave.* The most used verb in the English language is *to be*, and it's the most irregular of all. So Table 2-1 sets it out for you.

Verbs that end in *-ing* — *progressive tenses* — can cause problems. These tenses rely on the verb *to be*. Always take care to match the subject to the correct form of the verb *to be*. Examples are: *I am trying, we were trying, they had been trying, you will be trying.*

Another group of verbs (that possibly have fairly fat heads because they're called *perfect tenses*) contain forms of the irregular verb *to have*. Be careful to use the correct form of this irregular verb too. Examples are: *I have bitten*, you *have bitten*, Spike *has bitten*, we *have bitten*, the wombats *have bitten*.

Table 2-1   Singular and Plural Forms of the Verb 'To Be'

Tense	Singular	Plural
Present	I am	we are
	you are	you are
	he, she, it is	they are
Past	I was	we were
	you were	you were
	he, she, it was	they were
Future	I will be	we will be
	you will be	you will be
	he, she, it will be	they will be
Present perfect	I have been	we have been
	you have been	you have been
	he, she, it has been	they have been
Past perfect	I had been	we had been
	you had been	you had been
	he, she, it had been	they had been
Future perfect	I will have been	we will have been
	you will have been	you will have been
	he, she, it will have been	they will have been

Matching two subjects

Just as a sentence can have one subject matched with more than one verb, so too a sentence can have more than one subject matched with just one verb. Two (or more) subjects joined by *and* usually take a plural verb, even if each of the subjects is singular. (Think of maths: 1 + 1 = 2. One subject + one subject = plural subject.) Here's how it works:

> Gerard and the fairy belong together. (*Gerard* + *fairy* = plural subject, *belong* = plural verb)

> Ando and Johnno plan to gnome-nap Gerard. (*Ando* + *Johnno* = plural subject, *plan* = plural verb)

Looking like Verbs: Verbals

All sorts of words like to stay fit by functioning as several different parts of speech, depending on how they are used. *Verbals* may look like verbs, or even be part of a verb group, but on their own, they don't perform any verb jobs in a sentence. In this section, we look at the three key verb-impersonators.

The most important thing to know about verbals is this: when you ask the question to find the verb, don't choose a verbal as your answer. If you do, you'll miss the real verb or verbs in the sentence.

Participating with participles

Participles are actually parts of verbs (hence the amazingly original name) that are not directly connected to the subject of the verb. So, when participles appear without the support of auxiliary or helping verbs, they act as adjectives (modifying nouns and noun equivalents). Here's how to recognise one:

- Participles look like verbs and can indicate present or past. *Present participles* end with *-ing*: *coping*, *blushing*, *posing*. Some *past participles* end with *-ed* (those from regular verbs such as *coped*, *blushed*, *posed*). Some end with other letters (those from *irregular verbs* such as *driven*, *gone*, *broken*).

- They have auxiliary verbs. For example: *had been* trying, *is* taken, *was* stuck, *will be* completed.

Naming gerunds

Occasionally, those *-ing* participles from the preceding section like to function as nouns. When they do this, they're called *gerunds*. Sounds more like a little furry creature than a tricky two-timing verb form, doesn't it? All gerunds end in *-ing* — *swimming, dripping, fishing, dancing, singing* and so on.

Here are a few examples, with the gerund and all the words associated with it (the *gerund phrase*, in grammar-geekspeak) italicised:

> *Swimming* is not foremost in Midge's mind; he prefers *surfing.* (*swimming* = subject of the verb *is*; *surfing* = subject of the verb *prefers*)

> Bobo, a generous person in every other way, hates *sharing her food.* (*sharing her food* = object of the verb *hates*)

> The importance of *remaining calm* can't be overemphasised. (*remaining calm* = object of the preposition of)

One gerund-related and very old-school rule is still respected by some modern grammar checkers, but confuses many modern writers. It has to do with the way we use pronouns with gerunds. Here's an example:

> WRONG: I hope you don't mind me asking.

> RIGHT: I hope you don't mind my asking.

As for many grammar rules, this distinction is all but extinct in casual communication. It should still be applied, however, in formal written documents. Here's how it works.

In the preceding sample sentence, the *-ing* word is a gerund. It is doing the work of a noun. Let's substitute another noun in its place to prove it:

> I hope you don't mind my questions.

See? They mean exactly the same thing. The sentence doesn't ask whether you're disturbed by *me*. It asks whether you're disturbed by *the asking.* And that's the trick to trying to decide how to revise the sentence. Try replacing the pronoun in front of a gerund with the word *the*. If it sounds comfortable, your *-ing* word is doing the work of a noun; it's a gerund. The only pronouns you can legally use in front of a gerund are *my*, *your*, *his*, *her*, *their* or *our*.

Defining infinitives

The *infinitive* is the *base form of a verb* (the *to* form) but like a singer without a band, it can't do the job of a verb unless it's supported by auxiliary or helping verbs in a verb group. Infinitives look like verbs, with the word *to* tacked on in front — *to dance, to dream, to be, to dally* and so on.

The following examples of infinitives in their natural habitat, the sentence, may help you to identify them. The infinitive and the words associated with it (called the *infinitive phra*se in grammarspeak) are in italics:

> Lucinda *likes to spend*. (*to spend* = the object of the verb *likes*)
>
> *To sing on Australian Idol* is Willem's lifelong dream. (*to sing on Australian Idol* = the subject of the verb *is*)
>
> Macca's goal is *to be unemployed forever*. (*to be unemployed forever* = the subject complement of the verb *is*)

Back when brown cardigans were cool, it was considered a crime to split the infinitive. This 'rule' is a hangover from Latin-loving grammarians who insisted that because in Latin a to-infinitive was a single word (which, of course, couldn't be split), it must still never be split. And your 'I'm so up to date I'm going to let you break that old rule a little bit' computer may try to tell you that no more than one word should stand between the *to* and the verb part of a *to*-infinitive. However, the meaning of your sentence may depend on whether or not the 'rule' is applied.

Consider these examples:

> Gina expects *to* more than *double* her wealth monthly. (split)
>
> Gina expects more than *to double* her wealth monthly. (not split)

The first sentence means 'Gina looks forward to her bank balance increasing by at least the power of two every month' — *more than* is modifying *double*. The second sentence is saying 'Gina greedily anticipates even more than the monthly doubling of her bank balance' — *more than* is modifying *expects*. Not the same meaning at all. Sorry computer, epic fail!

Chapter 3

Completing Sentences

⊛ ⊛

In This Chapter

▶ Understanding the elements of a complete sentence

▶ Exploring clauses

▶ Identifying sentence fragments

▶ Completing ideas with objects and complements

⊛ ⊛

*P*ossibly the most basic rule of English grammar is that near enough is not good enough. Officially, all sentences must be complete.

But everyone breaks the rule. Often. Which may not seem fair. *Often* isn't a complete sentence. It's a *sentence fragment*. But you understood it, didn't you? (That's an incomplete sentence, like the opening to this paragraph.) In this chapter, you find out how to decide whether your sentence is grammatically complete, and how to identify some important elements of sentences: *clauses, objects* and *complements*.

Having Subject–Verb Pairs

A complete sentence must have at least one subject–verb pair. They're a pair because the verb has been adjusted to match with the subject (there's plenty about subject–verbs pairs in Chapter 2). And while we're getting technical, a verb that can be adjusted in this manner is called a *finite* verb. To be legal, a sentence must include one element expressing action or being (a verb), and one element that's performing the action or being (a subject). To make a correct pair, the verb must be written in a form that has a clear meaning when teamed with its subject. *They match* is a correct subject–verb pair with a clear meaning. But what if we said, *They to match*? You may be able to work out the meaning, but you can hear that the pair is not a proper team. Something is missing.

Some subject–verb pairs that match are

> The team (subject) has lost (verb).
>
> Some supporters (subject) will swear (verb) but others (subject) will sulk (verb).
>
> Sweaty sport socks (subject) smell (verb).

Just for comparison, here's one mismatch:

> The triumphant winners (subject) celebrating (verb).

The subject–verb pair doesn't match. The sentence doesn't make complete sense. Something is missing.

When you're checking a sentence for completeness, search for a matching subject–verb pair. If you can't find at least one, you don't have a complete sentence.

Complete sentences may match one subject with more than one verb, and vice versa:

> Ellie appeared in three commercials but sang in only two. (*Ellie* = the subject of the verbs *appeared* and *sang*.)
>
> Rusty and Fang fight endlessly over a bone. (*Rusty* and *Fang* = the subjects of the verb *fight*.)

Complete sentences that give commands may match an implied subject (*you*) with the verb:

> Send an email to everyone who left details. (*You* = the implied subject of the verb *send*; *who* = the subject of the verb *left*.)

(For a more complete explanation, refer to Chapter 2.)

Expressing Complete Thoughts

It's not enough for a sentence to begin with a capital letter
and end with a full stop. A complete sentence must express
a complete thought, like this:

> Despite Kylie's fragile appearance, she is a tough
> opponent.
>
> Danni planned her attack.
>
> She pounced.

Here are some incomplete thoughts, just for comparison:

> The reason I should be the star.
>
> Because I said so.

You may be thinking that both of the preceding incomplete
thoughts could be part of a longer conversation. Yes, you're
right. You can make these incomplete sentences grammatically
complete by stating the ideas that the rest of the conversation
gives you:

> I explained the reason I should be the star, even though
> she was really only interested in trying on her glittery
> costume.
>
> You have to clean up your desk because I said so.

So, now you know that every complete sentence must have at
least one subject–verb pair and express a complete thought.

Creating Completeness with Clauses

No matter what you put between two pieces of bread, you have
a sandwich. That's the definition of sandwich: bread plus filling.
Clauses have a simple definition too: subject plus *finite verb*
(a verb that has been adjusted to match its noun). A *clause* is a

complete unit of meaning within a sentence. Any subject–verb pair creates a clause. The reverse is also true: no subject or no verb — no clause. You can throw in some extras (descriptions, joining words, lettuce, tomato … whatever), but the basic subject–verb pair is the key. In this section, we look at how we use clauses to create complete sentences.

Understanding clauses

The simplest form of sentence is just one clause, but some sentences have multiple clauses. And some sentences are made up of a *main clause* and a *dependent clause* (or clauses).

Some sentences have just one clause — the whole sentence is the clause. This doesn't necessarily mean, however, that the sentence is very short because all sorts of other details can be added to the clause. Here are a few single-clause sentences:

> Rihanna sings. (subject = *Rihanna*, verb = *sings*)
>
> Has Hugh found the woman of his dreams yet? (subject = *Hugh*, verb = *has found*)
>
> Only the boy with the red hair and cheeky smile noticed her embarrassing slip on the dance floor. (subject = *boy*, verb = *noticed*)
>
> Jeff and his employees have reached a new pay agreement. (subjects = *Jeff* and *his employees*, verb = *have reached*)
>
> Gabrielle fixed the dripping tap and ordered a water tank. (subject = *Gabrielle*, verbs = *fixed* and *ordered*)

Note that one of these sentences has two subjects and one has two verbs, but each expresses just one main idea.

Here with more than one clause:

> SENTENCE: Tran had finished most of his homework, so his mother said that he could watch his favourite television show.
>
> CLAUSE 1: Tran had finished most of his homework (subject = *Tran*, verb = *had finished*)
>
> CLAUSE 2: his mother said that he could watch his favourite television show (subject = *his mother*, verb = *said*)

CLAUSE 3: that he could watch his favourite television show (subject = *he*, verb = *could watch*)

Telling main from dependent clauses

Some clauses are self-sufficient. They live alone without any problem. These are called *independent* or *main clauses*. Other clauses are like grown-up children who still live at home with their parents. They can't manage without support. These clauses are called *dependent* or *subordinate clauses*. (Both sets of terms are interchangeable.)

Both types of clauses, main and subordinate, have subject–verb pairs, but one big difference exists between them. Main clauses make complete sense on their own. Subordinate clauses don't.

Independently main clauses

Main or independent clauses are okay by themselves. They are complete. They can manage alone. Writing too many main clauses in a row, however (as we just did in these introductory sentences), can make your paragraph sound choppy and dull.

You can combine main clauses with other main clauses to make more appealing sentences. *Coordinating conjunctions* (the joining words *and, but, nor, so, yet*) are used to join main clauses to each other. When you do this, the message in each clause is of equal importance.

Here are some sentences to demonstrate the use of coordinating conjunctions:

SENTENCE: Bobo loves Luke *and* she likes him to cook their meals.

CLAUSE 1: Bobo loves Luke

COORDINATING CONJUNCTION: and

CLAUSE 2: she likes him to cook their meals

SENTENCE: She wanted duck à l'orange *but* he didn't know the recipe *nor* does he speak French.

CLAUSE 1: She wanted duck à l'orange

COORDINATING CONJUNCTION: but

CLAUSE 2: he didn't know the recipe

COORDINATING CONJUNCTION: nor

CLAUSE 3: does he speak French

Dependently subordinate clauses

Subordinate (or dependent) clauses aren't okay by themselves because they don't make complete sense. They're not complete sentences.

When her father wasn't looking

Because Grandpa Griswald thrives on caffeine

To become complete sentences, subordinate or dependent clauses need the support of main clauses (*subordinate* means secondary or lower in rank). To make complete sense, subordinate clauses have to be attached to main clauses; they depend on them for completeness.

Subordinate clauses often function as (do the work of) adjectives or adverbs to the main clause, adding more information. They don't carry the main message of a sentence. A subordinate clause all by itself is a grammatical crime in formal writing — a sentence fragment. (Stay tuned for more about sentence fragments in the following section.)

The best sentences combine different elements in all sorts of patterns (see Chapter 10 for more advice on how to build better sentences). In the following examples, the main clauses are combined with subordinate clauses to create longer, more interesting sentences:

Laura blasted Riley with her new water pistol when her father wasn't looking.

Because Grandpa Griswald thrives on caffeine, he was delighted to discover the packet of chocolate biscuits at the back of the cupboard.

Considering Fragments

A *sentence fragment* or *incomplete sentence* may look and sound like a sentence, but it doesn't have all the necessary elements to make it a legal sentence. Read on and you'll discover how to identify and correct any fragments you write.

Fragmented subject–verb pair

Listen to a conversation. People rarely speak in complete sentences. Consider the following:

> Where did you get that mud cake? (complete sentence)
>
> From the cafe next door. (fragment: no subject or verb; needs *It came* from the cafe next door to be complete)
>
> Looks delicious. (fragment: no subject; needs *It* looks delicious)

Sentence fragments often occur because the sentence doesn't have a complete subject–verb pair. (Remember them? Refer to Chapter 2 for detail on subject–verb pairs.)

Fragmented ideas

Another common type of incomplete sentence occurs when only part of an idea is communicated. If the first word is something like *and*, *but* or *because* (which are conjunctions), what follows is probably only half an idea. Conjunctions work like glue: they bind things together. Frequently, these words are used to combine two (or more) complete sentences (with two or more complete thoughts) into one longer sentence:

> Lucinda's mother was extremely thirsty, *but* she didn't like camomile tea *and* that was all Ms Stakes was offering her.

The example contains three sentences, joined by a *but* and an *and*:

> Lucinda's mother was extremely thirsty. She didn't like camomile tea. That was all Ms Stakes was offering her.

If you begin your sentence with a conjunction, what you're communicating may well fit the definition of a sentence (because it contains a subject–verb pair), but it can still be considered incomplete. Why? Because it only conveys part of the meaning. It's part of a longer sentence. Let's look at that incomplete sentence:

> Because it only conveys part of the meaning. (subject–verb pair = *it conveys*)

The subject–verb pair is present, but the idea is not complete. What's missing from this sentence is the first half. It's actually the end of the complete, longer sentence:

> It can still be considered incomplete because it only conveys part of the meaning.

It used to be a crime punishable by death to begin a sentence with a conjunction. Nowadays, writers commonly break this 'rule' and they don't spontaneously combust. But their computers probably caution them with the message 'Fragment (consider revising)' whenever they do it. Squiggly lines aplenty would draw attention to both of the following italicised groups of words:

> Marlo adores string concertos. *And plays violin.* (fragment)

> Marlo adores string concertos. *And she plays violin.* (incomplete sentence)

This is further proof that those bossy little grammar checkers are nowhere near as clever as we are. We know that the first example is a *fragment* of a sentence because it does not have a subject–verb pair. Who *plays*? No idea. However, the second example has the correct subject–verb pair *she plays*. If we remove the conjunction, a complete and correct sentence remains: *She plays violin.* See the difference? So the second example, although an incomplete sentence, is not a sentence fragment. Epic fail grammar checker!

That said, beginning a sentence with a coordinating conjunction is frowned upon in formal writing. So how do you revise your conjunction-caused incomplete sentence? Any of several ways is possible. You could:

- try putting the sentences together with the conjunction as the connector
- remove the conjunction
- completely reword the sentence
- create a stronger emphasis by using a different kind of connecting word such as *additionally, also, as well as, however, on the other hand* or *whereas.*

Remember, too, that the other reason your computer may highlight a sentence fragment is that the sentence lacks a subject–verb pair. To revise such sentences, you need to provide the missing piece of the pair, or perhaps even add a subject–verb pair.

Contemplating Complements

Cruising on the grammar highway, the sentence is a car carrying meaning to its destination: the reader. The verb is the engine and the subject is the driver. The object or the complement are common (but not always essential) parts of the car — perhaps the parking sensor or the towbar. They are, however, a little more important than a mirror on the sun visor. (Although it's a pretty close call!) You can create a sentence without an object or a complement, but its presence is generally part of the full driving — sorry, the complete *communicating* — experience.

So, sometimes all you need (because it says everything) is the subject and the verb:

> Nicole phoned.

And sometimes you need a bit more:

- ✔ Nicole was anxious.
- ✔ Nicole phoned Keith.
- ✔ Keith gave Nicole a single red rose.
- ✔ Keith called Nicole the love of his life.

Each of these four sentences begins with a subject and verb, and each has something more to complete the sentence. The other stuff is called the *complement*. (No, not compliment with an *i*, as in, 'Wow, that's the nicest sentence anyone's written this week'; complement with an *e*, which means *the part that completes something*.) Complements *complete* the sentence. Of course, that's not enough for grammarians. They can see that each of these sentences ends in a slightly different way and, if they can come up with four names instead of one, they will. So in this section, we look at the different kinds of sentence complements.

Receiving direct objects

An *action verb* expresses an action that's being performed by someone or something in a sentence and tells you something is happening or changing. (Chapter 2 deals with all sorts of verbs.) Sometimes, these verbs need something extra to tell the whole story. Check out this sentence:

> Nicole phoned Keith.

Here, *phoned* is an action verb because it expresses what's happening in the sentence. The action goes from the *subject* (*Nicole* — the person performing the action of the verb) to Keith. So in grammarspeak, this makes *Keith* the *object*. In other words, Keith directly receives the action of phoning. In even more specific grammatical terms, Keith is the direct object of the verb phoned. (He's also the object of Nicole's affections!)

Here are two more examples of sentences with direct objects:

> A flying skateboard shatters a window. (*skateboard* = subject, *shatters* = verb, *window* = direct object)

> Mum confiscated my skateboard. (*Mum* = subject, *confiscated* = verb, *skateboard* = direct object)

Of course, just to make your life a little bit harder, a sentence can have more than one direct object. Check out these examples:

> Keith autographs *CDs* and *photographs* for his admirers.

> Mum expects *honesty, politeness, respect* and unbroken *windows.*

Baring complete objects

Right about now you may be asking the very logical questions: What about the extra words around the object words? Why aren't they included? (A fine line exists between grammar-geek

and grammar-genius, and you're perilously close to the border!)
The reason has to do with the fact that the object of a verb is
always a noun or a noun equivalent — as is the *subject*. (Go
back to Chapter 2 without passing 'Go' if you've forgotten what
a subject is.) A *noun equivalent* is a word, or group of words,
that's doing the same work as a noun in the sentence. It may
be a pronoun, or a noun group. So the words italicised as the
objects in the preceding sample sentences are the nouns (not
the whole noun equivalent).

Those of us who are on intimate terms with objects like to call
the noun the *bare object* and the whole noun equivalent the
complete object. The following sentences help settle the score
in the matter of bare versus complete:

> Geeks wear *cardigans*. (*wear* = verb, *geeks* = subject,
> *cardigans* = object)

> Geeks wear *brown cardigans*. (Same verb, same subject,
> but an extra word is in front of the noun *cardigans*. The
> group of words, *brown cardigans*, is now doing the same
> job as the single noun, so *brown cardigans* is the kind
> of noun equivalent that can be called a *noun group*. It is
> also the complete object of the verb *wear*.)

> Geeks wear *incredibly daggy brown cardigans with
> baggy elbows*. (Same verb, same subject, same bare
> object, but lots of extra information in the complete
> object.)

Identifying the direct object or complement

In Chapters 1 and 2, we explain how to locate the verb by asking
the right questions. (*What's happening? What is?*) In Chapter 2,
we show you how to track down the subject. (*Who? What?* is
performing the verb.) In this chapter, you discover how to find

the direct object or the complement. To do so, first identify the subject–verb pair, and then ask these questions:

- ✔ Whom?
- ✔ What?

The reason that the question to ask yourself after the subject–verb is *Whom?* and not *Who?* is like the difference between *he* and *him* or *they* and *them.* The choice depends on whether the pronoun is performing the verb, making it a *subject pronoun,* or is affected by the action of the verb, in which case it's an *object pronoun.* (See Chapter 4 for more on pronouns as subjects and objects.) So, because we aim to promote best practice in grammar manners, we're going to stick with using the formal *Whom?* as our object question. If you do too, you'll never confuse *who* with *whom* again. Well, not once you've mastered the grammatical jobs of identifying subjects and objects.

Ask yourself the identifying questions in this sentence:

Max owns the cleanest car in town.

1. **Ask the verb question: What's happening?**

Answer: *Owns.* Owns is the action verb.

2. **Ask the subject question: Who or what *owns?***

Answer: *Max owns.* Max is the subject.

3. **Ask the object/complement question: Max owns whom or what?**

Answer: Max owns *the cleanest car in town* (the complete object). Because *car* is receiving the action of the verb, car is the direct object (the bare object).

Recognising indirect objects

Another type of object is the indirect object. This one is called *indirect* because the action doesn't flow directly to it. The *indirect object,* affectionately known as the IO, is like a pit stop between the action verb and the direct object. Consider this sentence, in which the indirect object is italicised:

Keith gave *Nicole* a single red rose.

The action is *gave. Keith* performed the action, so *Keith* is the subject. What received the action? The *rose.* Keith didn't actually *give* Nicole, he *gave* the rose. So, *rose* is the direct object. That's what was given; the rose received the action of the verb directly. But *Nicole* also received the action, indirectly. The rose was given *to* her. *Nicole* received the giving of the rose. *Nicole* is called the indirect object.

Here are a couple of sentences with the indirect objects italicised:

> Mum will tell *Dad* the whole ugly story tonight. (*will tell* = verb, *Mum* = subject, *story* = direct object)

> Tom promised *Katie* the world. (*promised* = verb, *Tom* = subject, *world* = direct object)

Indirect objects don't appear very often and, when they do, they're always in partnership with a direct object. You probably don't need to worry too much about them, as long as you understand that these words are objects that complete the meaning of an action verb, you can recognise the basic structure of a sentence.

Completing Linking Verbs

So far in this chapter, all the verbs we've discussed have been action verbs. 'What about the other category of verbs?' we hear you ask. Do they take objects too? What happens when the verb is not an action verb but a linking verb? Let's look at this sentence:

> Tom seems upset.

1. **Ask the verb question: What's happening or what is?**

   Answer: *Seems*. Nothing is happening in the sentence, but you do arrive at an answer for the *What is?* question. *Seems* is the linking verb.

2. **Ask the subject question: Who or what *seems*?**

   Answer: *Tom seems*. Tom is the subject.

3. **Ask the object/complement question: *Tom seems* whom or what?**

   Answer: *Upset*. So *upset* is the object, right? Wrong! *Upset* is not an object, even though it completes the sentence and follows the verb. Upset is the *complement* of the linking verb *seems*.

Let's run that past you again. What follows a linking verb looks like an object, and acts like an object, but is not an object. What follows a linking verb is called a *subject complement*. Why does it have a different name? Well, oddly enough, the explanation is simple: a complement following a linking verb expresses something about the *subject* of the sentence. So, when grammar-geeks talk about 'the complement', this is the one they mean, the one that completes a linking verb. Look at these:

> The dog was *happy* until the skateboarding incident. (dog = happy)

> Natasha used to be a *rocket scientist*. (Natasha = rocket scientist)

> It is *I*, the master of the universe. (It = I)

Sometimes the subject complement is a descriptive word (an *adjective*), like *happy* in the first sentence in the preceding list. Sometimes the subject complement is a *noun* (person, place, thing or idea), like *rocket scientist*. And sometimes it's a *pronoun* (a word that substitutes for a noun) like *I*.

Complementing the Object

Sometimes a direct object doesn't get the whole job done. A little more information is needed (or just desired), and the writer doesn't want to bother adding a whole new subject–verb pair. Look at this sentence:

> Keith called Nicole the love of his life.

Keith isn't phoning Nicole, he's saying something about her. *The love of his life* finishes the sentence, so it's some sort of complement, right? It's called an *object complement* because it adds more information about the direct object. The object complement may be a person, place or thing (a *noun*), as in the previous example. It may also be a word that describes a noun (an *adjective*; see Chapter 5 for more information). Take a peek at this sample:

> Nicole called Tom *heartless*. (*called* = verb, *Nicole* = subject, *Tom* = direct object)

As you see, the object complement comes after the direct object. It gives the sentence a little more flavour. But the object complement is not a major component of the sentence.

Chapter 4

Peaking with Pronouns

*M*any long years ago, in a land where men were chivalrous and ladies all wore dresses, one would always place oneself last in the sentence, speaking thusly: 'Wouldst anyone care to come a-wassailing with Lord Jagger, Sir Bob and I?'

The people of the kingdom were committing unpardonable sins in the use of pronouns. So, their error was passed down the lines of their descendants verily unto the modern day.

Yes, choosing the correct pronoun can be tricky, even for those who can wield a sword or ride side-saddle. *Pronouns* are words that substitute for nouns. English has many different types of pronoun, each governed by its own set of rules. In this chapter, we concentrate on how to avoid the most common errors associated with this class of words.

Matching Pronouns with Nouns

Pronouns stand in for other words. So, to choose the appropriate pronoun, you must consider the word that the pronoun is replacing (which is called the pronoun's *antecedent* — a name meaning 'going before'). Here's a look at how this works:

> Millie Magpie fed *her* chicks the delicious sausage *she* stole from the barbeque below *her* nest. (The pronouns *her* and *she* stand in for the antecedent *Millie Magpie*.)

> Johnno, *who* hates a beer, tried to convince *his* new wine-snob boss to order a keg for the staff party. (The pronouns *who* and *his* stand for the antecedent *Johnno*.)

 You should be able to replace the pronoun with its antecedent (or the antecedent with the pronoun) without changing the meaning of the sentence.

Avoiding Vague Pronoun Use

The best way to remain clear in your use of pronouns is to keep the pronoun and its antecedent close to each other. Vague use of pronouns can confuse your reader or listener. Check this out:

> Costa had hay fever. He pulled out his handkerchief. He blew his nose. Yasmin had given it to him — the love of his life. He was terrified of losing her. He sniffed. It was always worse when he walked through the park. She was a treasure.

This example has more than one problem. *Yasmin* is too far from *she*, and we have no idea what's worse when Costa walks through the park, his hay fever or his emotional state. (And did she really give him his *nose*?) Here's one possible revision:

> Costa had hay fever, and it was always worse when he walked through the park. He pulled out his handkerchief. Yasmin — the love of his life — had given it to him. She was a treasure. He was terrified of losing her. He sniffed and blew his nose.

Now the antecedents and pronouns are closer to each other. Much better!

While it's true that a pronoun is more likely to be understood if it's placed near the word it replaces, position isn't always enough, especially if more than one antecedent is possible. Look at this sentence:

> Lucinda told her mother that she was out of cash.

Who's out of cash? The sentence has one pronoun (*she*) and two nouns (*Lucinda* and *Lucinda's mother*). *She* could refer to either of them. The antecedent is not clear. The best way to clarify the meaning of a pronoun is to make sure that each pronoun represents only one easily identifiable antecedent. If readers can interpret the sentence in more than one way, rewrite it:

> Lucinda was out of cash so she told the sad tale to her mother.

or

> Lucinda saw that her mother was out of cash and told her so.

Choosing Singular and Plural Pronouns

All pronouns are either singular or plural. *Singular* pronouns replace singular nouns, which are those that name *one* person, place, thing or idea. *Plural* pronouns replace plural nouns — those that name *more than one* person, place, thing or idea. Logical enough, right? So just to make things crystal clear, Table 4-1 lists some common singular and plural pronouns.

Table 4-1	Common Singular and Plural Pronouns
Singular	**Plural**
I	we
me	us
myself	ourselves
you	you
yourself	yourselves
he/she/it	they/them
himself/herself/itself	themselves
who	who
which	which
that	that

Pairing Pronouns with Collective Nouns

Collective nouns (orchestra, committee, team, squad, army, class and the like) refer to groups and can present a problem when choosing the right pronouns (and verbs).

Collective nouns exist because these groups often act as a unit, doing the same thing at the same time. If that's the case, treat the noun as singular and make sure that the pronouns that refer to it are also singular. Like this:

> The audience rises and is ready to leave as soon as the concert ends.

So, if the audience is a unit, would the audience clap *its* hands or *their* hands? Let's see:

> The audience rises and is ready to leave as soon as *it* has finished clapping *its* hands. (Oh dear.)

The audience doesn't share two big hands. You can safely assume that 99.7 per cent of audience members have two individual hands each. So how do you fix the problem? Dump the collective noun and substitute the plural *members of the audience*:

> The members of the audience rise and *are* ready to leave as soon as *they have* finished clapping *their* hands.

Members is now the subject. *Members* is plural, so the verbs (*are, have*) and pronouns (*they, their*) are all plural too.

To sum up the general rules on pronouns that refer to groups:

✔ Treat collective nouns as singular if the group is acting as a unit.

✔ Some collective nouns may take singular or plural pronouns and verbs, but do not mix the two for the same collective noun — especially not in a single sentence.

✔ If the members of the group are acting as individuals, you can use a plural verb, but it's better to switch the collective noun for a plural noun.

No matter what you might see (or hear) on websites, in advertisements, on billboards and even in mail, company names are always singular and so must take singular pronouns and verbs. Yes, even if the company name ends with an *s*, and even if the company employs half the planet. For example:

> *Eccentric Electronics is* moving *its* operation.

> *Catherine's Cookies has* crumbled and closed *its* doors.

Selecting Pronouns as Subjects

The subject is the person or thing that is 'doing' the action of the verb (or 'being' the verb if it's a linking verb). (For more on locating the subject, refer to Chapter 2.) You can't do much wrong when you have the actual name of a person, place or thing as the subject — in other words, a noun — but pronouns are another story.

The following can help you to remember which are the only legal subject pronouns.

Subject Pronouns	*Object Pronouns*
I, you, he, she, it	me, you, him, her, it
we, they	us, them
who, whoever	whom, whomever

Here are some examples of pronouns as the subject of a sentence:

> Actually, *I* did once ride a horse side-saddle. (*I* is the subject of the verb *did*.)

> *Whoever* marries Damian next should have her head examined. (*Whoever* is the subject of the verb *marries*.)

Matching more than one subject

Most people can manage one subject, but sentences with two or more subjects (*compound subjects*) can be tricky. For example, you often hear otherwise grammatically correct speakers say things like

> *Him* and *me* are going to get some fish and chips.

> Damian and *me* had met before.

See the problem? In the first example, the verb *are going* expresses the action. To find the subject, ask *who* or *what are going?* The answer right now is *him and me are going*, but *him* isn't a subject pronoun. Neither is *me*. Here's the correct version:

> *He* and *I* are going to get some carrots and celery. (We couldn't resist correcting the nutritional content too.)

In the second example, the action — the verb — is *had met*. *Who* or *what had met?* The answer, as it is now, is *Damian and me*. *Me* is not a legal subject pronoun. The correct version is

> Damian and *I* had met before.

 A good way to check your pronoun use in sentences with more than one subject is to look at each one separately. You may have to adjust the verb a bit when you're speaking about one subject instead of two, but the principle is the same. If the pronoun doesn't work as a solo subject, it isn't right as part of a pair either. Here's an example:

ORIGINAL SENTENCE: *Lucinda* and *me* went shopping in the sales yesterday.

CHECK: *Lucinda* went shopping yesterday. Verdict: no problem.

CHECK: *Me* went shopping in the sales yesterday. Verdict: problem. Substitute *I*.

CHECK THE REVISED VERSION: *I* went shopping in the sales yesterday. Verdict: that's better.

COMBINED, CORRECTED SENTENCE: *Lucinda* and *I* went shopping in the sales yesterday.

Selecting pronouns as objects

Previously in this chapter, we've concentrated on subject pronouns, pronouns that perform the action of the verb, but now it's time to focus on the receiver of the sentence's action — the object. Specifically, it's time to examine *object pronouns*. (For more information on finding the object, refer to Chapter 3.) Pronouns that may legally function as objects include *me, you, him, her, it, us, them, whom* and *whomever*.

Here are some examples of object pronouns, all in italics:

Dad took *us* to the new movie despite its dreadful reviews. (*Took* is the verb; *Dad* is the subject; *us* is the object.)

Someone sent *me* a very obscure *text message*. (*Sent* is the verb; *someone* is the subject; *text message* and *me* are objects.)

Knowing Who or Whom

Knowing whether the pronoun is being used as a subject (*who*) or an object (*whom*) is the sure-fire, grammar-buff-approved way of choosing between the pronouns *who/whoever* and *whom/whomever*. Another way is to apply 'the *m* rule'. Try substituting the pronouns *him* or *them* (both of which end with the letter *m*) for the pronoun in your sentence. If the sentence sounds comfortable, choose the pronoun that ends with an *m* and use *whom.* Like this:

> You sent on my email joke to *whom?* (You can substitute *him* or *them* and the sentence is fine. *He* or *they* would not work.)
>
> And *who* advised you to do that? (You can substitute *he advised* or *they advised* and the sentence makes sense, but *him advised* or *them advised* do not.)

Comparing with Pronouns

Being busy, we take short cuts, chopping words out of our sentences and racing to the finish. This practice is evident in *comparisons.* Read the following sample sentence:

> Charlene denied that she had more facial hair than he.

That sentence really means

> Charlene denied that she had more facial hair than he had.

If you say the entire comparison like this, the pronoun choice is easy.

 Whenever you have a comparison that the sentence suggests but doesn't state completely — finish the sentence in your head. The correct pronoun becomes obvious. Better still, finish it in your sentence as well — it will sound much more natural.

> No-one gave Charles as much trouble as she (did).

Owning Possessive Pronouns

Possessive pronouns show (pause for a drum roll) *possession.* Not the head-spinning-around, projectile-vomiting kind of possession, but the kind where you own something. Check out the following:

> Sure that *his* phone had beeped *its* last beep, Shane shopped for a new one.

The possessive pronouns in this example show that the beep belongs to the phone and the phone belongs to Shane.

Possessive pronouns also have singular and plural forms. You need to keep them straight. Table 4-2 helps you identify each type.

Table 4-2	Singular and Plural Possessive Pronouns
Singular	**Plural**
my	our
mine	ours
your	your
yours	yours
his/her/hers/one's	their/theirs
its	their
whose	whose

Putting an apostrophe into the possessive pronoun *its* is a very common error, and your computer often highlights it for you to check. *It's* does not mean *belongs to it*. *It's* means *it is*. Always. Without exception. *It's* and *its* work like this:

My computer exploded and *its* RAM is more random than ever before. (belonging to *it*)

It's raining data in here. (it is)

It's been a while since I backed up the hard drive. (it has)

One's is the only possessive pronoun that ever has an apostrophe, and unless you live in that quaint land referred to at the start of this chapter, you probably never use *one's* anyway.

Reflecting on Reflexive Pronouns

In this era of self-interest, *reflexive pronouns* (also called the *-self pronouns*) get quite a workout. Just as a mirror reflects an image back to you, so a *reflexive pronoun* reflects another word (a noun or noun equivalent) used earlier in the sentence. The reflexive pronouns are *myself, yourself, himself, herself, itself, oneself, ourselves, yourselves* and *themselves*. Here are some of them at work:

> Lucinda's parents blamed *themselves* for her selfishness. (*themselves* refers back to the noun group *Lucinda's parents*)

> She behaves *herself* only with difficulty. (*herself* refers back to the pronoun *she*)

The word to which any pronoun refers back is called its *antecedent*. With *reflexive pronouns*, the antecedent is always the subject of a verb.

A second legitimate use for these self-confident pronouns is to emphasise or focus on something specific about the word to which the reflexive pronoun refers back (its antecedent). Some picky grammarians call this same group of pronouns *intensive pronouns* because they intensify the point being made about the subject of the verb, like this:

> Tex *himself* will be playing guitar on my new song. (And we all know what a hot guitarist Tex is.)

> I mowed the grass *myself*. (Even though I've never done it before but I was sick of waiting for you to do it.)

Some people consistently use reflexive pronouns incorrectly (probably because they think it sounds more formal).

> WRONG: Please address your response to Charlotte and *myself*.

> RIGHT: Please address your response to Charlotte and *me*.

Sentences such as the preceding example require a pronoun from the object list (*address your response* to whom? *address your response* to me) not a reflexive pronoun.

Chapter 5

Modifying with Descriptions

*W*ith the right nouns (names of people, places, things or ideas) and verbs (action or being words) you can create a pretty solid, but basic, sentence. In this chapter, we explain the two main types of descriptive words of the English language — *adjectives* and *adverbs* — and show you how to use each correctly to add meaning and interest to your writing. We also demonstrate how to avoid placing a description in the wrong spot.

Adding Meaning with Adjectives

If you've ever wished that a writer would stop describing the scenery and get on with the story, you probably think that descriptive words just hold up the action. But sometimes they can be the key to expressing your meaning. Take a look at this sentence:

> Lucinda was sauntering through Westfield when the sight of a Ferragamo Paradiso paralysed her.

Would you understand this sentence? What do you need to know in order to make sense of it? Apart from the meaning of words like *saunter* (which you could look up in a dictionary if you weren't sure what it meant), you'd need some background information. For example:

- ✔ Westfield is a shopping centre. (You probably do know that.)

- ✔ Ferragamo is an expensive shoe label. (Maybe you know that.)

- ✔ A Paradiso is a type of shoe. (You couldn't know that because we made it up.)

It would also help to know that Lucinda is obsessed with shoes. If you knew all this, or if you have a good imagination and the ability to use context clues when reading, you probably understood it.

But what if you didn't know all this to start with? That's when descriptions can be useful. Here's version two:

> *Shoe-obsessed* Lucinda was sauntering through *consumer-oriented* Westfield when the sight of a *fashionable, green, high-heeled evening* sandal with the *ultra-chic* Ferragamo label paralysed her.

Okay, it's overloaded a bit, but you get the point. The descriptive words help to clarify the meaning of the sentence, particularly for the fashion-challenged.

Now that you realise that descriptions can be essential to the meaning of a sentence, we know you're dying to find out more. Read on.

Describing with Adjectives

An *adjective* is a descriptive word that *modifies*, or adds more detail, about a noun or a pronoun. It adds information about colour, type and other qualities to your sentence.

Where do adjectives hang out? Most of the time you find them in front of a noun (the one the adjective is describing), but they roam about a bit. You may find them after the noun or after a pronoun (when they're describing the pronoun). And sometimes you find them connected to their noun by a linking verb. We consider all these ways of using adjectives in turn, but first a quick look at how to spot an adjective.

Locating adjectives

To locate adjectives, go to the words they modify (nouns and pronouns). Find the noun and ask these questions:

- ✔ Which one?
- ✔ What kind?

Take a look at this sentence:

Magneto placed the short red wires in his new invention.

You see three nouns: *Magneto, wires* and *invention.* You can't find answers to the questions *Which Magneto?* or *What kind of Magneto?* The sentence doesn't give that information; no adjectives describe *Magneto.*

But try the questions on *wires* and *invention* and you do come up with something. What kind of wires? Answer: *Red* and *short.* *Red* and *short* are adjectives. The same goes for *invention.* What kind? Answer: *New. New* is an adjective.

Adding adjectives to nouns

The most common job for an adjective is adding to the meaning of a *noun* — describing a noun. Here are some sentences with the adjectives in italics:

There is a *poisonous* snake on your shoulder.

There is an *angry venomous* snake on your shoulder.

There is a *rubber* snake on your shoulder.

All the adjectives are describing the noun *snake* and they're all in front of the noun. In these three sentences, those little descriptive words certainly make a difference. They give you information that you would really like to have. See how diverse and powerful adjectives can be?

Now here's an example with the adjectives after the noun:

> Kyle, *sore* and *tired*, pleaded with Sandy to release him from the headlock she had placed on him.

Sore and *tired* tell you about *Kyle*. Note that when more than one adjective is used after a noun they need to be joined by an *and*. You can't just say *Kyle, sore tired* (*sore* seems to be describing *tired* rather than *Kyle*). If you use more than two adjectives, you should punctuate them like a list. (We cover punctuating lists in more depth in Chapter 6.) Here's an example using three adjectives after the noun:

> Kyle, *sore, tired and thirsty*, pleaded with Sandy to release him from the headlock she had placed on him.

If you can put the word 'and' between the adjectives, you can separate them with a comma. You could have *sore and tired and thirsty*. But look at this example:

> Jess chose a *fresh, fruity white* wine to have with her Thai takeaway.

You could say *a fresh and fruity white wine* but you wouldn't say *a fresh and fruity and white wine*. *White* is not just describing *wine*; the adjective is actually defining the noun. *White wine* is a particular type of wine, not just a description of the wine's colour. Look at another one:

> Kris closed the *large, steel garage* door onto the bonnet of Eva's new car.

The last comma has been omitted from the list of adjectives in the last sentence because *garage* is defining *door*. In fact, defining adjectives couple so closely with their noun partners that they almost form a compound noun. That's how language changes. A defining adjective and a noun get so attached to each other that they decide to link up with a hyphen. Pretty soon they can't bear that distance either, and so they drop their hyphen and become permanently attached as a single word, while legions of stickler grammar-geeks weep into their handkerchiefs. For example, *back yard* morphed into *back-yard* before reinventing itself as *backyard*.

Adding adjectives to pronouns

Adjectives can also modify or tell you more about *pronouns* — they can describe pronouns (words that substitute for nouns):

> There's something *strange* on your shoulder. (The adjective *strange* describes the pronoun *something*.)

> Everyone *conscious* at the end of the play made a quick exit. (The adjective *conscious* describes the pronoun *everyone*.)

As you can see, these adjectives usually go after their pronouns.

Using adjectives with linking verbs

Adjectives may also follow *linking verbs*, in which case they describe the subject of the sentence (which can, of course, be a noun or a pronoun). Linking verbs join two ideas, associating one with the other. They're like equals signs, equating the *subject* (which comes before the verb) with another idea that comes after the verb. (Refer to Chapter 2 for full details of linking verbs.)

Sometimes a linking verb joins the subject to an adjective (or a couple of adjectives):

> The afternoon appears *dull* because of the nuclear fallout from Winston's cigars. (The adjective *dull* describes the noun *afternoon*.)

> Now the car is *bent* and *sad*. (The adjectives *bent* and *sad* describe the noun *car*.)

You'll notice that an *and* appears between the adjectives *bent* and *sad* when they come after a linking verb (just as it does when two or more adjectives come *after* a noun).

Describing with Adverbs

Adjectives aren't the only descriptive words. *Adverbs* are also descriptive words. These words modify the meaning of a verb, an adjective or another adverb. Check these out:

> The boss *regretfully* said no to Rashid's request for a raise.

> The boss *furiously* said no to Rashid's request for a raise.

> The boss *never* said no to Rashid's requests for a raise.

If you're Rashid, you care whether the word *regretfully*, *furiously* or *never* is in the sentence. *Regretfully*, *furiously* and *never* are all adverbs. In this section, we examine how adverbs describe or add meaning to other words, but first we need to make sure you know how to recognise an adverb when it's occupied in a sentence.

Finding adverbs

Adverbs mostly modify verbs, giving more information about an action. Nearly all adverbs (enough so that you don't have to worry about the ones that fall through the cracks) answer one of these four questions:

- ✔ How?
- ✔ When?
- ✔ Where?
- ✔ Why?

To find the adverb, go to the verb and ask yourself the questions directly after the verb. (Refer to Chapter 2 for information on finding the verbs.) Look at this sentence:

> 'I've finally solved the mystery of the book,' said the sergeant excitedly, as he was just going.

First, identify the verbs: *solved* and *said.* Then ask the questions. Solved when? Answer: *Finally. Finally* is an adverb. Solved how? Solved where? Solved why? No answers. Now for *said*. Said how? Answer: *Excitedly*. *Excitedly* is an adverb. Said where? Said when? Said why? No answers. And finally, *was going*. Was going how? No answer. Was going when? Answer: *Just*. *Just* is an adverb. Was going where? No answer. Was going why? No answer. The adverbs are *finally*, *quickly* and *just*.

Adverbs can be in lots of places in a sentence. If you're trying to find them, rely on the answer to your questions *how*, *when*, *where* and *why*, not the location of the word in the sentence. Similarly, a word may be an adverb in one sentence and something else in another sentence. Check these out:

> Lucinda went *home* in a huff.
>
> *Home* is where the heart is.
>
> *Home* movies are Mildred's specialty.

In the first example, *home* tells you where Lucinda went, so *home* is an adverb in that sentence. In the second example, *home* is a place, so *home* is a noun in that sentence. In the third example, *home* is an adjective, telling you what kind of movies they are.

Using adverbs to describe other describing words

Adverbs also describe, or modify, other descriptions, usually making the description more or less intense. (A description describing a description? Give me a break! But it's true.) Here's an example:

> Nicole was extremely unhappy when Keith didn't phone her.

How unhappy? Answer: *Extremely unhappy*. *Extremely* is an adverb describing the adjective *unhappy*.

Sometimes the questions you pose to locate adjectives and adverbs are answered by more than one word in a sentence. In the previous example sentence, if you ask *Was when?* the answer is *when Keith didn't phone her*. Don't panic. These longer answers are just different forms of adjectives and adverbs. A group of words can do the job of an adjective or adverb in a sentence, just as a group of words can do the work of a noun or a verb. There's more about that later in this chapter. Now back to work. Here's another example:

> Nicole quite sensibly put it out of her mind and reorganised her bank accounts.

This time an adverb is describing another adverb. *Sensibly* is an adverb because it explains how Nicole *put*. In other words, *sensibly* describes the verb *put*. How sensibly? Answer: *Quite sensibly*. *Quite* is an adverb describing the adverb *sensibly*, which in turn describes the verb *put*.

In general, adverbs that describe adjectives or other adverbs won't give you much trouble.

Using adverbs to modify a complete statement

One humble adverb that receives far too much attention, especially from grammar checkers that aren't set correctly, is *hopefully*. Back when cocky was an egg, the only acceptable meaning for *hopefully* was *in a hopeful way* or *with hope*. Like this:

> Hopefully, I waited for my team to win a premiership. (*hopefully* is modifying the verb *waited* to tell you how *I waited*.)

But for decades, the most common use of hopefully has carried a more general meaning, something like *it is hoped*. Like this:

> Hopefully, the top team will lose.

What is the adverb modifying here? Not the verb *will lose*. (Teams don't lose in a hopeful way!) *Hopefully* is modifying the whole statement, and the speaker is allowed to do that. The statement is expressing something about the attitude of the speaker, not about the subject of the sentence. We can use other adverbs in this way. *Luckily*, *sadly* and *honestly*, for example, don't attract the accusing squiggly line from a grammar checker. So why is *hopefully* singled out in this way? It's time to end the persecution of this simple adverb.

If your computer tells you to consider revising a sentence in which *hopefully* is used in the second way, mumble something about how ironic it is that you have a computersaurus-rex trying to tell you — a breathing, thinking grammarphile — how to use an adverb correctly, and switch off the grammar-check function for a while.

Misplacing Descriptions

Can you spot what's wrong with this sentence?

> Steve put a ring into his freshly pierced lip that he bought last week.

The way the sentence is now, *that he bought last week* describes *lip*. You can buy all sorts of cool and weird things on eBay, but not lips (yet). Here's the correction:

> Steve put a ring that he bought last week into his freshly pierced lip.

Now, *that he bought last week* follows *ring*, which Steve really did buy last week.

The description *that he bought last week* is a group of words that modifies the noun *ring*. Often, groups of words starting with *that*, *which* or *who* modify or add more information to a noun or noun equivalent.

Here's another description that wandered too far from home:

> Barbie bought a genuine, 1950-model, fluorescent pink hula-hoop with a credit card.

According to news reports, toddlers and dogs have received credit card application forms, but hula-hoops haven't — at least as far as we know. How to fix it? Move the description:

> Using a credit card, Barbie bought a genuine, 1950-model, fluorescent pink hula-hoop.

Granted, most people can figure out the meaning of the sentence, even when the description is in the wrong place. The human brain is a wonderful thing. But a real danger exists that occasionally you'll write a sentence that doesn't say what you mean.

The rule concerning description placement is simple: place the description as close as possible to the word that it describes.

Dangling a Description in Space

Taking short cuts saves time and energy, and you likely do it all the time when you communicate. You leave words out and assume that the listener or reader is going to be able to supply the missing piece. But what happens if the information isn't where we expect it to be? Read this sentence:

Scoffing a sausage roll, the cholesterol really builds up.

Who is eating the sausage roll? In this sentence, no-one is scoffing. We don't know who the subject is for that part of the sentence.

What about this example?

Watching the football on TV, Carla caught Eddie breaking his diet.

You're waiting to find out who's watching the match and ... there's the answer, the nearest subject: Carla. Well, no, actually it was Eddie who was watching the match when Carla came in unexpectedly and caught him binging on chips and beer. So what's going on in these sentences?

Verb forms are hanging around not connected to anything, dangling subject-less. Verb forms that have nothing appropriate to describe are called *danglers* or *dangling modifiers* (or *hanging* or *misrelated* or *unattached modifiers* — nothing excites grammar-geeks more than term proliferation). Dangling modifiers latch on to the nearest possible subject and make it their own. To correct the sentences, make sure that the subject is right there where you need it:

Carla caught *Eddie* breaking his diet while he was watching the football on TV.

OR: *Eddie* was watching the football on TV when Carla caught him breaking his diet.

Dangling descriptions kidnap the first thing they find and force it to act as their subject. For those of you who are enjoying life as a trainee grammar-guru, the problem word is often a *participle* (an *-ing* form or *-ed* form of a verb). So, watch out if any of your sentences start with an *-ing* word and make sure that you're saying what you mean.

A dangler can also be an *infinitive* (*to* + a verb) that begins a sentence:

WRONG: To avoid eye strain, Clare bought her staff bigger computer screens. (Who's avoiding eye strain? Clare? No. She's the boss and already has a massive screen. It's the staff who've been squinting at monitors.)

RIGHT: So that they wouldn't strain their eyes, Clare bought her staff bigger computer screens.

ALSO RIGHT: To prevent them straining their eyes, Clare bought her staff bigger computer screens.

Remember that you fix a dangler by making sure that you have a clear subject–verb pair.

Danglers can also lead to your grammar checker warning you that you have written a passive sentence that you should consider revising. (Chapter 10 contains all the ins and outs of passive and active voice.) The error message is telling you that your sentence lacks a subject performing the action of the verb. In fact, your sentence may not have a subject at all. Here's an example:

To learn about grammar, read this book.

Who is doing the learning and the reading? Ummm? Well, nobody specific is performing the verbs in this sentence, but it implies two possible subjects: you or everybody. It's an imperative (a sentence that gives an instruction or general advice), which may be exactly what you intended. To revise, decide whether you need to add a subject to a passive sentence or if you intended the subject to be vague.

Squinting Descriptions

Some descriptions cause confusion because they sit between two things they could modify and look both ways without latching on to a specific word. Take a look at the following example:

> The workmate Robbo annoyed often gave him a warning.

Exactly what does the sentence mean? Did Robbo *often annoy* the workmate? Or perhaps the workmate *often gave* Robbo a warning.

The problem is that *often* is between *annoyed* and *gave* and can be linked to either of them. The sentence violates a basic rule of description: don't put a description where it can have two possible meanings. Descriptions that look over both shoulders at words they could modify are called *squinting modifiers*.

How do you fix the sentence? You move *often* so that it's closer to the verb it should be modifying, thus showing the reader which of the two words it describes. Here are two correct versions of the previous example, each with a different meaning:

> The workmate Robbo often annoyed gave him a warning. (*Often* clearly belongs to *annoyed*, so Robbo was behaving badly again and his workmate finally flipped and gave him a warning.)

> The workmate Robbo annoyed gave him a warning often. (Now *often* clearly belongs to *gave*. The workmate has decided not to take anything from that little smart alec, and gives Robbo a warning every time he even looks like stepping out of line.)

The most common modifiers to commit the crime of squinting are single words: *only*, *just*, *almost* and *even*. (See Chapter 8 for more about where to place these words.)

Chapter 6

Punctuating for Meaning

*Y*ou don't need to be a construction expert to know that a building requires more than steel, timber and bricks. A plethora of little things — nails, bolts, mortar, rivets — also complete the structure and make it strong. The same is true of good communication. So in this chapter, we explain the rivets and bolts of writing: commas, apostrophes, quotation marks, semicolons, colons and dashes. By the end of this chapter, you'll understand how punctuation is an essential part of the communication-building process.

Conquering Commas

Commas break your sentences into chunks to help you communicate your exact meaning. The key is to put the commas where they help the reader to see and hear the sense of the sentence. The rules concerning commas aren't hard to understand, so forward ho!

Using commas in lists

The shopping list says: torch batteries butter shortbread ice-cream cake. So how many things do you have to buy? Perhaps only three: torch batteries, butter shortbread, ice-cream cake. Or maybe six: torch, batteries, butter, shortbread, ice-cream, cake. No, it's four: torch batteries, butter shortbread, ice-cream, cake. How do you know? You don't, without the commas. So, here's what you need to buy, listed in a sentence:

> You need to buy torch batteries, butter shortbread, ice-cream and cake.

You need commas between the items in the list, with one important exception: you don't need one between the last two items. Why? Because the *and* is separating the last two items. But if you want to throw in an extra comma there, you can. It's not wrong. It's your choice.

The comma that comes before the *and* in a list of three or more items is so famous that it has its own name. It's called the *serial comma* or the *Oxford comma*. You don't need to remember what this list comma is called, but you do need to know how it can help you communicate more clearly.

Look at this sentence:

> Gemma did her school project about the explorers Leichhardt, Burke and Wills and Eyre.

If you didn't know that Burke and Wills belong together as a team, and Eyre worked solo, you might be confused. But, if you didn't, you might be confused. To be clear, this sentence needs the serial comma before the *and*:

> Gemma did her school project about the explorers Leichhardt, Burke and Wills, and Eyre.

To avoid confusion, in case the reader links the explorers into pairs, it's best to put the serial comma in this version too:

> Gemma did her school project about the explorers Burke and Wills, Leichhardt, and Eyre.

So the general rule here is this: if an item in the list already has an *and*, put a comma before the *and* between the last two items. You don't have to put a comma before the *and* in every list.

Stringing adjectives together

To add personality and interest (and sometimes maybe even to stretch the truth), you enrich your sentences with *adjectives* and *adverbs*. (For more information on adjectives and adverbs, refer to Chapter 5.) Now look at the descriptions in the following sentence:

> When Mark dressed Ella in the outfit her grandparents had given her, she looked like a toddling frilly pink cushion.

No commas separate the three descriptive words in the sentence: *toddling, frilly* and *pink*. Using commas in lists of adjectives is not essential. It's a choice. So, the following tip sets out how to use them legally with adjectives if you choose to do so.

If you can put *and* between the adjectives comfortably, without disrupting the meaning of the description, it's okay to add a comma if you wish. So in the preceding example you'd get *a toddling* and *frilly* and *pink* cushion (which all sounds comfortable, so the commas are okay). But never put a comma between an adjective and the noun it's modifying.

Sometimes one descriptive word is clearly more important than the rest. All the descriptive words in a sentence may not deserve equal emphasis. Take a look at this example:

> Lucinda just bought a funny, little, cocktail hat.

Here, you're giving equal weight to each of the three descriptions. Do you really want to do so? Probably not. Instead, you're likely to be emphasising that it's a *cocktail* hat. (Who buys cocktail hats these days?) So, you don't need to put commas between the other descriptions and would write it as 'a funny little cocktail hat'.

Using commas with determiners

Check out this sentence:

> 'I still have two big presents to save for,' said Maria.

No commas are used in *two big presents*. Would it be legal to write *two, big presents*? No. Why not? No comma appears after *two* because numbers are a different kind of modifier from descriptive adjectives. In grammarspeak, numbers are *determiners*. They give you different information (how many presents or which presents, not what sort of presents). Try adding *and* between the words to hear this more clearly.

> I've got two *and* big presents.

See, it doesn't work, does it?

Don't use commas to separate determiners from the words that they modify or from other descriptive words. (*Determiners* go in front of a noun and tell you how specific or otherwise something is — refer to Chapter 1 for more information).

Addressing people directly

Traditionally, whenever you address someone directly, you need to separate the person's name from the rest of the sentence with a comma. Otherwise, your reader may misread the intention of the message. Take a look at the following:

> I gave the hinglefluber to your brother, Frank.
>
> I gave the hinglefluber to your brother Frank.

The first sentence is addressing Frank, and Frank has a brother who has the hinglefluber. In the second sentence, Frank has the hinglefluber.

In line with the trend to keep punctuation as uncomplicated as possible, this rule is being relaxed a little. So, in a short sentence, especially in an informal communication like a note or a personal email, you can drop the comma. Like this:

> 'Thanks Frank.'
>
> 'Hi Clare.'

Noting introductory and concluding words

Sometimes, people set up what they're about to say with a word or two (as this sentence demonstrates). At other times, people tack some extra words on the end of a sentence. But how do you punctuate introductory or concluding elements? Read on.

Firstly, use a comma to separate introductory or concluding words from the rest of the sentence if the meaning of the sentence is not changed when you omit the extra element. Read these examples twice, once with the extra words and once without. See how the meaning stays the same?

> I don't like your attitude, no.
>
> Loud and over-confident, Jodie dominated the conversation.

Secondly, words that link a sentence to the idea that follows or precedes it are best set apart from the rest of the sentence with commas:

> For instance, Frank's hinglefluber could prove to be a useful deterrent.
>
> We may use it to keep Mildred's snake at bay, for example.

Thirdly, an element that modifies the whole sentence is separated from the rest of the sentence with a comma. Like these:

> Unfortunately, your garment was eaten by the tumble dryer.
>
> Your white shorts are now pink, apparently.

If, however, your sentence contains an element that can't be removed without changing the meaning of the sentence, the comma is optional. You can choose whether or not to use it.

> Yesterday the rules seemed so much clearer.
>
> Yesterday, the rules seemed so much clearer.
>
> The rules seemed so much clearer yesterday.

In some situations, however, leaving the comma out can confuse the reader. Consider this sentence:

> After winning his head grew even fatter.

Did you read *After winning his head* as the introductory element? Adding the comma leaves no room for confusion. The reader pauses at the comma and the meaning is clear:

> After winning, his head grew even fatter.

To sum up, use a comma to separate an introductory or concluding element from the rest of the sentence if that element can be removed from the sentence without changing the meaning, if it connects ideas, or if it modifies the whole sentence. Otherwise, you can leave it out unless its omission creates confusion for the reader.

Adding extra detail with pairs of commas

When you add information that's not strictly necessary into a sentence, you need a pair of commas to mark off that extra information from the rest of the sentence. This includes descriptions and further explanations, as well as words that are interruptions to the main sentence — words such as *therefore*, *of course* and *by the way*. Consider the following sentences with and without commas:

> Politicians, who gather information from social media, are not to be trusted.

> Politicians who gather information from social media are not to be trusted.

What's the difference? In sentence one, *who gather information from social media* is a description of *politicians*. It's extra information. So, it's set off from the rest of the sentence by commas. You can take it out and the sentence still means the same thing — *Politicians are not to be trusted*. None of them. Not ever. And, by the way, they all use social media as a source of information. But do not trust them.

Without the commas, as in the second example, the information becomes essential to the meaning of the sentence. It can't be removed without altering what you're saying. Without commas, the description changes the subject of the sentence from the noun *Politicians* to the noun group *Politicians who use social media*. It gives the reader essential information about the meaning of *politicians* in this sentence. This sentence is warning that you can trust some politicians but not others. Do not trust the ones who gather information from social media.

Remember that commas travel in pairs as far as extra information is concerned. Don't use just one comma where you need two. When reading over what you've written, stop at the commas to check whether the information that follows can be removed from a sentence. If it can, put another comma at the end of the information.

Never put a comma between a subject and its verb, even if the subject is really long. Look at this sentence:

> RIGHT: The guy who I met last night at the tram stop carries a purple man-bag.

> WRONG: The guy, who I met last night at the tram stop, carries a purple man-bag.

The first sentence is correct because the subject that matches the main verb of the sentence (*carries*) is *The guy who I met last night at the tram stop*. The second sentence is wrong because, if you take out the information between the commas, the sentence doesn't easily make sense. It becomes *The guy carries a purple man-bag*. What guy? The complete subject no longer comes before the verb.

Connecting commas with conjunctions

When you join two complete sentences with the conjunctions *and, or, but, nor, yet* or *so*, it can help your readers if you put a comma before the conjunction. However, it is not essential and the comma is usually omitted if the sentences being joined are short. Here are some examples:

> Mike may tell Susie when they have dinner together next week, or he may tell her today.

> Mike may tell her tonight or he may remain silent.

The rule of never putting a comma between a subject and its verb also applies with sentences that have one subject (who or what you're talking about) and two verbs joined by *and, or, but, nor, yet* or *so*. Don't put commas between the two verbs. You aren't joining two complete sentences, just two words or groups of words. Here are two examples:

> WRONG: Susie said nothing, but stared very loudly.

> WHY IT'S WRONG: The sentence has one subject (*Susie*) that has two verbs (*said* and *stared*). You aren't joining two complete sentences here, so you shouldn't place a comma before the conjunction (*but*).

> RIGHT: When Mike told Susie, Susie said nothing but stared very loudly.

Airing All about Apostrophes

Apostrophes are those high-flying commas that hang around the tops of letters. They're also the most misused and abused of all punctuation marks. Fear not. In the following sections, we explain how to avoid apostrophe catastrophes.

Using apostrophes in contractions

A *contraction* shortens a word by removing one letter or more and substituting an apostrophe in the same spot. For example, chop *wi* out of *I will*, throw in an apostrophe, and you have *I'll*. The resulting word is shorter and faster to say.

Take a look at Table 6-1 for a list of common contractions. Note that some are irregular. (*Won't*, for example, is short for *will* not.)

Table 6-1		Contractions	
Phrase	*Contraction*	*Phrase*	*Contraction*
are not	aren't	she would	she'd
cannot	can't	that is	that's
could not	couldn't	they are	they're

Phrase	Contraction	Phrase	Contraction
did not	didn't	they will	they'll
do not	don't	they would	they'd
does not	doesn't	we are	we're
he had	he'd	we had	we'd
he is	he's	we have	we've
he will	he'll	we will or we shall	we'll
he would	he'd	we would	we'd
I am	I'm	what has	what's
I had	I'd	what is	what's
I have	I've	who has	who's
I will or I shall	I'll	who is	who's
I would	I'd	will not	won't
is not	isn't	would not	wouldn't

Owning apostrophes of possession

English gives you two ways of indicating ownership or possession: with or without an apostrophe. For example:

the house of my friend = my friend's house

the letters of the lovers = the lovers' letters

the fine wines of that corner bar = that corner bar's fine wines

To use the possessive apostrophe correctly (to mean 'belonging to'), first decide whether the noun is singular (one) or plural (more than one), then add the apostrophe. Doing so helps to ensure that the s and the apostrophe are in the correct order — *friend's house* is singular. *Lovers' letters* is plural.

Showing ownership with singular nouns

To show possession by one owner, here's the rule: first add an apostrophe and then the letter *s* to the owner. Examples are:

> The *dragon's* claws (The claws belongs to the dragon.)
>
> *Captain Cavity's* gold-filled tooth (The gold-filled tooth belongs to Captain Cavity.)

Another way to think about this rule is to see whether the word *of* expresses what you're trying to say. Check these examples:

> the cover *of* the atlas = the *atlas's* cover
>
> the long memory *of* the elephant = the *elephant's* long memory

Showing ownership with plural nouns

The plurals of most English nouns — anything greater than one — already end in *s*. To show ownership, all you do is add an apostrophe after the *s*. Take a look at these examples:

> four *dogs'* muddy paws (That's 16 muddy paws belonging to four dogs.)
>
> the *dinosaurs'* petrified eggs (The petrified eggs belong to the dinosaurs.)
>
> the 12 *roses'* fading petals (The fading petals belong to the 12 roses.)

In Australia, we don't use apostrophes in place or street names. So you'll find names like *Flinders Street, Kings Cross, St Patricks Place* and *Berrys Beach*.

Companies, shops and other organisations also own things, so these proper nouns (nouns that begin with a capital letter) also get apostrophes. Put the apostrophe at the end of the name. For example:

> *Heinz's* 57 varieties
>
> *RM Williams'* boots

You can sometimes avoid the whole problem of the apostrophe by thinking of the owner as a sort of adjective instead: *Heinz varieties, RM Williams boots, Telstra profits.* This doesn't always work, but it can get you out of some tricky situations.

Irregular plural possessives

Of course, not all plural English words end in *s.* Lots of them are irregular. To show ownership for an irregular plural (one that doesn't end in *s*), add an apostrophe and then the letter *s.* Like this:

> the *children's* pet mice (The mice belong to the children.)
>
> the *mice's* feet (The feet belong to the mice.)

Compound plural possessives

An apostrophe can apply to a whole group of words (not just the one it's connected to). For example:

> *Keith, Nicole, Sunday Rose and Faith's* house (The house is home to all of them.)

However, if two people own things separately, as individuals, you should use two apostrophes to make this clearer:

> Her *sister's* and *Jacque's* cars were parked outside. (Two people, two cars.)

Collective noun possessives

Some nouns are used to indicate a collection or group, like *team, herd* and *army. Collective nouns* stand for more than one object, but you should treat the group as one thing. So:

> The *team's* defeat
>
> The *school's* reputation.

Remember that an apostrophe shows ownership. Don't use an apostrophe when you have just a simple plural (a word that's *not* expressing ownership). Here are some examples:

> RIGHT: Tomatoes aren't to everyone's taste.
>
> WRONG: Tomatoe's aren't to everyone's taste.

Possessives with hyphens

For words with *hyphens* — son-in-law, mother-of-pearl, 20-year-old — the rule is simple: put the apostrophe at the end of the word, never inside it. For example:

> the *dogcatcher-in-chief's* canine teeth (The canine teeth belong to the dogcatcher-in-chief.)

> the *doctors-of-philosophy's* common room (The room is for the use of all the doctors-of-philosophy.)

Possessives ending in s

Singular nouns that end in *s* present special problems. Jimmy Barnes has recorded a lot of songs, but the name *Barnes* is singular, because he is only one person. Hence:

> I love Jimmy *Barnes'* raspy style.

or

> Jimmy *Barnes's* screaming is not singing.

Both of these sentences are grammatically correct (whether or not you agree with the opinions they express). Why? Firstly, it has to do with sound. If the letter *s* crops up too many times, the words can be hard to say (and you can find yourself hissing and spitting all over your listener). Secondly, some grammarians assert that if a name has only one syllable and ends with *s*, you should add only an apostrophe.

Others, like us, prefer to go with the KISS principle rather than complicate the issue. We're big fans of an 'always rule'. So if you always add an apostrophe plus another *s* to a singular name, whatever letter it ends with, you'll always be right.

Leaving apostrophes out with possessive pronouns

English also supplies pronouns — words that take the place of a noun — for ownership. Here are some possessive pronouns: *mine, yours, his, hers, its, ours* and *theirs*. None of these possessive pronouns ever has an apostrophe.

> WRONG: Each dog has it's own favourite chair.

> RIGHT: Each dog has its own favourite chair.

For more information on possessive pronouns, refer to Chapter 4.

Simplifying Semicolons

Think of the highest selling series of books for the past century. No, nothing to do with the colour grey! Remember that boy wizard? *Harry Potter* reaches readers aged 8 to 80, and these novels are littered with colons and semicolons. Truly. You don't need to be a wizard to use them correctly.

Hinging complete thoughts

A semicolon (;) can join one complete sentence to another. It's a stronger piece of punctuation than a comma, but not as strong as a full stop. Think of a semicolon as a hinge connecting two sentences. An example:

> Stevo broke a bootlace; he went to the shop.

You can't just join any two sentences in this way. The sentences that semicolons join must relate logically to each other. (You wouldn't hinge the door to the window frame!) Look at this sample:

> Stevo broke a bootlace; he loves his job.

It's hard to see the connection between these ideas. The two ideas would be better expressed in separate sentences.

Joining with conjuncts

Conjuncts are transition words that help create a logical connection between ideas. The most common conjuncts are *however, consequently, also, moreover, therefore, nevertheless, besides, thus, indeed, still, otherwise, similarly, for example* and *for instance*. Conjuncts provide links, but they're not real conjunctions. So, you need to understand how they co-exist with semicolons. For instance:

> When the Lonely Hearts Club caught fire, Mr Kite ushered everyone outside; however, Maxwell rushed into the burning building to rescue his silver hammer.

Or this:

> When the Lonely Hearts Club caught fire, Mr Kite ushered everyone outside. Maxwell, however, rushed into the burning building to rescue his silver hammer.

In the first sample, two complete sentences are connected by *however*. So, it has a semicolon before it and a comma after it. In the second sample, the *however* is perfectly correct with a comma on either side of it because it isn't trying to join two sentences together.

If you use conjuncts improperly, your grammar checker may become unhinged. Leave out the accompanying semicolon when you use a conjunct as a link between two complete sentences and, in grammarspeak, they become a *run-on sentence*. To revise this sentence error, if you want to keep the *conjunct*, add a semicolon. Alternatively, you can replace the conjunct with a real conjunction (such as *because, so, but*), or make two sentences.

Separating in lists

The rule for semicolons in lists is very simple: when any items in a list include commas, separate all the items with semicolons. Even put a semicolon between the last two items on the list (before the conjunction).

Clarifying Colons

Here is the most frequent use of colons these days — gasp! :-0 open mouth of shock. Traditionally, though, a colon (:) like its younger sibling the semicolon, shows up when a simple comma isn't strong enough to connect ideas. A colon draws attention to the material that follows it. It is used to introduce information that develops or explains the words preceding the colon.

Setting up long lists

The colon precedes the first item of a lengthy list. Like this:

> Lucinda's list of things to do in her life included the
> following: work for a major fashion designer, buy a small
> island, have a big white wedding, star in a reality series
> and see all her diamonds being cut.

The words before the colon should form a complete thought.
If you put a colon in front of a list, check the beginning of the
sentence to be sure it makes complete sense on its own.

Setting up extracts

Use a colon before a long extract or quotation taken from
somewhere else. Such extracts are called *block quotes*. So here's
how you'd punctuate a review of Tiffany's new novel:

> I found some of the writing to be so sugary sweet that I
> feared it would give me cavities. Passages like this made
> me want to suck a lemon:
>
> > Candy was looking forward to another wonderful
> > day in Treacle Town. The new job excited her
> > so. The warmth of her new colleagues made
> > her smile on the inside even bigger than the
> > gorgeous glowing grin she showed the world.

Notice, too, that the block quote is set-in (indented). Throughout
this book we use a colon when we introduce sample sentences
and examples. They're being treated like block quotes.

Expanding on an idea

In one special situation, colons show up inside sentences, joining
one complete sentence to another or perhaps to a sentence
fragment (a piece of a sentence). When the second idea explains,
restates or summarises the meaning of the first idea, you may
join the ideas with a colon. And you can do this whether the
information following the colon is a complete sentence or just a
sentence fragment. Like this:

> Jude has a problem: he doesn't know how to improve his
> sad song. (two sentences)

> Jude sings only one kind of song: sad. (sentence + fragment)

If you've neglected to switch your grammar checker from its American default to Australian English, it may try to tell you that you always need to use a capital letter after a colon. This message is wrong. In Australian English, there are only three situations in which a colon may be followed by a capital letter:

- ✔ if the word following the colon is a proper noun

- ✔ in headings within a document

- ✔ for the first word of a subtitle.

Dealing with Dashes

You may not even realise that punctuation aficionados enjoy using dashes of three different lengths (although one is called a hyphen and not a dash). Read on and be amazed.

Using the humble hyphen with words

Here's a simple rule concerning hyphens: if two words are being used as a single description, put a hyphen between them if the description comes before the word that it's describing. That is, if the words are being used as an adjective. For example:

> We need a long-term solution.

but

> We can't go on doing this in the long term. (Because *long term* isn't describing anything here, it's a noun, not an adjective.)

The issue is ambiguity. If we had written *long term solution*, you may be confused about whether the solution is *long-term* or is it a long *term-solution*? The hyphen makes the meaning clear: *long* is describing *term*. You don't need to hyphenate two-word descriptions if the first word is an adverb (most of these end in -*ly*), because rarely any ambiguity exists:

fully understood idea

completely ridiculous grammar rule

You can't have a *fully idea* or a *completely rule* so it's obvious what the meaning is.

Well also causes problems sometimes. Follow the same rule here. Use a hyphen if it's part of a word that comes before the word it's qualifying, and leave the hyphen out otherwise. So:

I like a well-placed hyphen.

That hyphen is well placed.

Words made up of more than one part are called *compound* words. Hyphens separate parts of some compound words, such as *ex-wife*, *pro-choice*, *one-way*, *passer-by* and so forth. Don't put a space before or after the hyphen.

You can use a hyphen to create exactly the right combination of words to express your thought. You might want to create a *never-before-seen* adjective to describe that *hard-to-explain* thing. You can do it with *annoying-but-ever-so-useful* hyphens!

Sometimes it's difficult to know whether a compound is two separate words, two words connected with a hyphen, or just one word — *car park*, *car-park* or *carpark*. Often this is the process that words go through when they change. If you don't know whether a particular expression needs a hyphen, check a current Australian dictionary.

Using the humble hyphen with numbers

Another common use of hyphens is with numbers:

- ✔ Hyphenate all the numbers from twenty-one to ninety-nine.

- ✔ Hyphenate all fractions used as descriptions (*three-quarters full*, *nine-tenths finished*).

✔ Don't hyphenate fractions preceded by *a* or *an* (*a half of his brain, an eighth of an octopus*).

✔ Use hyphens where numbers and words are combined into an adjective (*19-year-old genius, ten-year-old wine, two-part series, three-ring circus*).

Use hyphens when you talk about someone who is *a 12-year-old* or *an 80-year-old*. Why? Because the term is still being treated as an adjective or determiner, even though a noun doesn't follow it. You're talking about *a 12-year-old child* or *an 80-year-old person*. Even though the last word (the noun) isn't said, it is understood. Don't use a hyphen, however, if you're using just the number as a determiner: *12 years old, 80 years young*.

Embracing Em and En Dashes

Dashes can look like this (—) or like this (–). The long dash is called an *em rule* or *em dash*. (*Rule* is just printer- and editor-speak for *line*.) The short one is called an *en rule* or *en dash*. They're so named because originally the em rule was as wide as a capital M and the en rule was as wide as an N. Each one of these dashes has a particular use.

An em rule can be set with or without a space on each side. It's a style choice. You'll notice that in this book we use the spaced em dash — an elegant, easy-to-read choice!

Em dashes tell the reader that you've jumped tracks onto a new subject for a moment. They can add extra information in the middle of a sentence (in which case you need a pair of dashes, just as you would need a pair of brackets or commas) or they can add something on the end (in which case, you need only one dash). Here are some examples:

> After we take the dogs for a good long run — I forgot to tell you about my greyhounds — we'll stop at the pub.

> Vicky was nearly killed when crossing the road last night — by a pair of speeding greyhounds.

An en dash is pretty technical. It has three main uses:

- ✔ to link spans, such as numbers in addresses, distances or times (*12–14 Station Street, aged 8–10, June–July, Sydney–Hobart yacht race*)

- ✔ to connect words that have a clear association, but where each retains its exact meaning and separate identity when joined (*hand–eye coordination, the Asia–Pacific region, Queensland–Northern Territory border*)

- ✔ to join names to indicate that you're talking about more than one person (*Costanza–Seinfeld effect, Cooper–Hoffstader theory*).

Dashes should be used sparingly. If your writing contains a lot of dashes, it is often a sign that your sentences are too long for readers to understand easily. Edit!

Chapter 7

Choosing Capital Letters and Numerals

* *

In This Chapter

▶ Understanding when capitals are required (and when they're not)

▶ Choosing between numerals and words

* *

*W*hen you write a text to a mate, you probably don't bother to use capital letters, and when you're busy at the keyboard, your word processor probably pops a few in for you as you type. But what do you do when you're updating your CV or editing a document that will reflect on your ability to use 'proper English'? Well, naturally, you flip open this trusty little reference book at the appropriate page and follow our advice. In this chapter, we cover a few of the stickier points of capitalisation to help you impress with accuracy. We also give you some pointers on numbers — in particular, how to decide whether to use numerals or words.

Covering the Basics of Capitalisation

Fortunately, the basic rules for capital letters are easy:

- ✔ begin every sentence with a capital letter
- ✔ capitalise the pronoun *I*
- ✔ begin quotations with a capital letter unless you're jumping to the middle of a quotation.

Don't change anything to a capital that's been deliberately named with a lower case letter, though. For example, internet addresses are almost always in lower case, you'll find poems attributed to an American poet known as e. e. cummings, some brand names reject capital letters and Daniel Johns and friends named their band silverchair.

Speaking officially

Meet *Mr* George Robinson, a *director* of a small local printing firm. George has aspirations to be *Lord Mayor of Sydney*. Mind you, next year, the *Archbishop of Sydney* also plans to run for the local council. His sister is pleased that George may be a *councillor*, but hopes he'll never be *Governor General*. Now what's going on with the capitals? Here are some general rules:

- ✔ Abbreviated titles (*Mr*, *Mrs*, *Miss* and *Ms*, but also *Dr*, *Prof.*, *Rev.* and so on) are always capitalised because they're attached to names. (If they are used alone, they're usually written out as, for example, *mister* and *missus*.)

- ✔ Titles like *director* and *councillor*, which refer to lots of people (more than one director exists and more than one councillor), are capitalised if associated with a name but not if on their own. (So you'd write *Lieutenant Jones*, but he's been promoted to the rank of *lieutenant*.)

- ✔ Titles that belong to only one person at a time (for example, the Secretary-General of the United Nations, the President of the United States, the Prime Minister of Australia and the Premier of Queensland) are capitalised when you're referring to one particular holder of the title. They're not given capitals when you're referring to the positions in a general way. (So you'd write to the Minister for Planning to complain that other *ministers* are contradicting what he's said.)

Addressing family

The rule for capitalising the titles of family members is simple. If the title takes the place of a name (as in *Grandma* instead of *Gladys*), capitalise it.

> Bill's brother Mike took their cousin's son to the zoo. (*Brother* and *cousin* are general kinship labels, not names, in this sentence.)

> He was embarrassed when Grandma Robinson saw him waddling past the penguin pool. (*Grandma Robinson* is a specific name.)

 Try substituting a real name for the family label in your sentence. If it fits, you need a capital letter. Let's substitute the name *Zeke* for the kinship label *dad* to see how this works:

> RIGHT: I told my *dad* that I was leaving.

> WEIRD: I told my *Zeke* that I was leaving.

> WRONG: I told my *Dad* that I was leaving.

See? So you don't need the capital letter in the sample sentence because *dad* cannot be replaced by his name.

Capitalising directions

Deciding whether to use a capital letter for the names of the points of a compass can cause confusion. A rough guide is that if you're talking about a specific part of the world, capitalise the words *North*, *South*, *East* and *West* but use lower case if you're just talking about a direction.

Another general rule is that, if one of these words is used as an adjective, sometimes the phrase becomes recognised as a geographical entity (South Korea, West Africa or the North Shore, for example) and then the adjective is capitalised. Otherwise, it isn't (eastern Sydney, northern Australia).

The names of other, smaller areas are often capitalised too. Melbourne has a South Bank. New York has a West Side. London has an East End. These have capital letters because they're the names of specific parts of the city.

Understanding geographical capital letters

Generally, the names of countries and cities, the languages spoken there, and the nationalities and ethnicities of the people who live there take capital letters. So you're pretty safe if you use a capital for any word that expresses direct connection with a place.

You should also capitalise locations within a country when the proper name is given (the name of a suburb or region, for example). Be sure to capitalise the entire name. Here are some examples:

- ✔ the Bungle Bungles
- ✔ Pakenham Upper
- ✔ the River Murray.

When the name doesn't appear, use lower case for geographical features such as *mountain*, *valley*, *gorge* and *beach*.

Is *the* part of a geographical name? Usually not, even when it's hard to imagine the name without it. In general, don't capitalise *the*.

A few countries have kindly lent their names to common objects: *French fries*, *Scotch whisky*, *Dutch oven*. Most people (and dictionaries) capitalise these. Some of these terms, however, have become so commonly used that they no longer refer to things with a direct connection to that place. So, their capital letter has been lost: *roman type*, *venetian blinds*. You need to check your trusty, up-to-date, Australian dictionary to be sure which ones need capitals.

You need to be extra-careful when discussing race and ethnicity. Black and White (or black and white) are acceptable, but be consistent. Don't capitalise one and not the other. It's best to refer to Indigenous Australians, sometimes also called Australian Aborigines, as Aboriginal and Torres Strait Islander peoples. Some people make the mistake of thinking Koori/Koorie has the same meaning as Aboriginal (*Koori* is a broad term for Aboriginal people of New South Wales and Victoria).

Talking about history

If you had a time machine, where would you go? Would you set the dial for the *Bronze Age*, *Middle Ages* or the middle of the *Dreaming*? You should probably select a *period* that didn't involve a *war*: the *Second World War* may be interesting to historians, but it wasn't much fun to live through. How about the *19th century*? Or the *Depression*? Perhaps you're really only interested in the *Eureka Stockade*.

The preceding paragraph should make the rules concerning the capitalisation of historical events and eras easy. Capitalise the names of specific time periods and events but not general words. Hence:

> ✔ capitalised: Bronze Age, Dreaming, Second World War, Depression, Eureka Stockade
>
> ✔ lower case: period, war.

 Everyone capitalises the Second World War, but some people call it World War II or WW2. Be consistent: don't mix and match.

Referring to times and times of year

After reading the following example, you can probably figure out the rule for using capitals with seasons and times without help:

> Lochness hates the *summer* because of all the tourists who try to snap pictures of 'an imaginary monster'. She's been known to roar something about '*winter's* peaceful *mornings*', even though she never wakes up before *1 pm*. Lochie especially loves *the winter solstice* and *leap years*.

Write the seasons of the year in lower case, as well as the times of day. Poetry is an exception, but everyone knows that poets make up their own rules, so those exceptions don't count.

When writing times, the abbreviation *am* stands for *ante meridian*, when the sun hasn't yet reached its highest point (the *meridian*). *Ante* is Latin for *before*. The other term — *pm* — stands for *post meridian*, when the sun has passed its highest point in the sky. *Post* is Latin for *after*.

Some people like to separate these time abbreviations with full stops, but Australian style is to leave out the full stops. Put a space between the number and the abbreviation. So you should write:

> 8.00 am, 9.52 pm, 11 am

Looking at titles

Bella is planning a party to celebrate the release of Stephanie's latest novel, *INDIGO DUSK: A TALE OF LOVE AND WEREWOLVES* (at least that's the way its name looks in the design on the cover). She is procrastinating about sending the invitations because she can't decide how to capitalise the title. What should she do? Well, that depends whether she wants to go for minimal capital letters (the KISS principle), in which case she'd only use capitals for the first word and any proper nouns in the title. (Notice also that titles are written in italics.) So it'd be:

> *Indigo dusk: a tale of love and werewolves*

Or, if she wanted to go for maximum effect with maximal capital letters, she would use a capital letter for the first word of the title, the first word of the subtitle, plus any other word that's not an article, preposition or coordinating conjunction. (Refer to Chapter 8 for more on prepositions.) So she would write:

> *Indigo Dusk: A Tale of Love and Werewolves*

Whichever style she chooses, it's important that she's consistent.

When writing the title of a magazine or newspaper, should you capitalise and italicise the word *the*? The answer used to be: 'Yes', if *the* is part of the official name, as in *The Age*; 'No', if the publication didn't include *the* in its official name, as in the *Mercury*. Now, however, it's increasingly more common in Australia not to bother at all.

Official Australian style suggests that you should use *The* with the title if it doesn't overlap with use of the ordinary word *the* in your sentence. Here's how it works:

> Julia read something surprising in the editorial of *The Canberra Times.*

> Julia read something surprising in the *Canberra Times* editorial.

In the first sentence, *The Canberra Times* is given as the name of the paper containing the editorial, and you don't need another *the* in front of it. While in the second sentence, what we mean is 'in the *The Canberra Times* editorial'. Only we're not actually saying that in as many words, because it would be silly to have *the The*. So, we drop *The* from the title of the newspaper and just use the ordinary definite article *the* in our sentence. Get it?

Descriptions of eras are sometimes shortened to capital letters such as *BP* (*before present*), *CE* (*of the common era*), *BC* (*before Christ*) and *AD* (*anno Domini*, which is Latin for *in the year of our Lord*). Put these forms after the year being discussed, but leave a space. And do not add full stops. Don't use capitals for writing the name of a century or decade. So:

> 55 BC, 1877 AD, the second century BC, 18th century, the sixties

Deciding When to Use Numerals

Obviously, when you write addresses, phone numbers and dates, you're going to use figures (or numerals). That's pretty obvious. What's not so obvious is choosing whether to write other numbers in numerals or in words. The choice is a matter of style, not of grammar. So your style manual or the authority figure in your life — tutors, bosses, probation officers or whatever — can tell you what they prefer.

For example, the preferred style of the *For Dummies* series is to use numerals for numbers above ten. So if we go just a little higher, we get to 11. Some organisations elect to use words for any number that can be expressed in fewer than three words. So they spell out one hundred (two words) but switch to figures for 101 (four words).

Australian style recommends that you spell out numbers below 100 if they're not a key focus of what you're writing, and use words up to nine and numbers thereafter if figures feature heavily in your document. So, if you're writing a novel, the likelihood that the text will be thick with numbers is slight and you can apply the 'words up to ninety-nine' rule. If, however, you're preparing a report of a survey conducted at a local farmers' market, you apply the 'words up to nine' rule. Whichever system you use, be consistent. Here are a couple of examples.

> Of the 178 people surveyed, only 16 had attended more than 10 times before. ('words up to nine rule')

> Of the eighty-seven people surveyed, only sixteen had attended more than ten times before. ('words up to ninety-nine rule')

The preceding pointers are style guides, not 'always' rules. Sometimes, you may have to break the rule in order for your sentence to be consistent. Consider the following sentence in that report of a farmers' market we mentioned earlier in this section:

> INCONSISTENT: The 87 people who attended specifically to purchase homemade dim sims ate an average of three each.

> CONSISTENT: The 87 people who attended specifically to purchase homemade dim sims ate an average of 3 each.

> ALSO CONSISTENT: The eighty-seven people who attended specifically to purchase homemade dim sims ate an average of three each.

Similarly, if a number begins a sentence, you must use words. And try to avoid ending a sentence with a numeral as well. You may also need to write out a fraction (for example, *four-fifths*) or any number that's an approximation (for example, *about three hundred*).

Chapter 8

Avoiding Tricky Situations

*S*o what's the point of all this proper grammar and precise punctuation anyway? Well, although it can't come up with ideas for you, good grammar creates no confusion for your audience when you communicate those ideas. Clear and accurate writing conveys the same (or as similar as possible) information to every reader. This book provides you with knowledge about some of the core skills of effective communication. It also helps you develop your skills as a critical reader and editor. In this chapter, we look at ten areas of grammar that commonly trip writers up. Eliminate these stumbling blocks from your writing — or check for them when you edit — and you'll be ahead of the pack in the race for success.

Eliminating Sexist Pronouns

Language is a very powerful tool. Publishers of books like this one edit them to eliminate any language that's racist, sexist, ageist or any other *-ist*. Whatever you think about equality, it's an important issue. And it affects pronouns (remember that a pronoun is a word that stands in for a noun; see Chapter 4 for more about pronouns).

Consider this sentence:

> A doctor is no longer expected to visit *his* patients at home.

We aren't talking about a specific doctor here. This is any doctor — a *typical* doctor — who treats *his* patients. How can you avoid suggesting that no doctors are women?

> A doctor is no longer expected to visit *his or her* patients at home.

That's clumsy, isn't it? And it makes *her* sound like an afterthought. Try a different pronoun:

> A doctor is no longer expected to visit *their* patients at home.

Well, no. That sentence doesn't exactly work either because a plural pronoun *their* is matched with a singular *noun* (a doctor). Although some people support this sort of mismatching on the grounds that it's not sexist, better ways exist to avoid this problem:

> *Doctors* are no longer expected to visit *their* patients at home. (Make the whole thing into the plural, then the gender-neutral *their* is correct because it's also plural.)

> A doctor is no longer expected to visit *patients* at home. (Leave the pronoun out.)

Your computer is likely to draw attention to potential problems with the mismatched pronouns we're talking about in this section. To revise a sentence that mismatches a singular pronoun with a plural one, you can rewrite the sentence to omit one pronoun or revise the sentence so that it is all plural. But what do you do if neither of those techniques works? Look at this sentence:

No-one should have to feel that *their* life is at risk. (*no-one* = singular, *life* = singular, *their* = singular?)

The sentence, as it stands, is fluent, clear and natural-sounding. How, then, could we revise it?

> *People* should not have to feel that *their lives* are at risk. (*people* = plural, *their* = plural, *lives* = plural)

Although the meaning is basically the same, the emphasis of the sentence is lost. It no longer speaks about each person as an individual, so it no longer addresses each reader personally. It just lumps everyone into one big pile of humanity.

The burning issue here is not whether pronouns like *no-one*, *everyone* and *anybody* are singular or plural. They're singular. No argument about that. It's whether *they*, *them* and *their* can be singular. And despite what those old-fashioned grammar nuts who resist change in language would have you believe, a long unbroken history exists of these pronouns being used as singular in written English. William Shakespeare did it. Jane Austen did it. You can even find it done in the Bible. So, as long as your sentence absolutely can't be successfully revised in *any* of the ways we've suggested, you have permission to use *they*, *them* and *their* as singular pronouns — judiciously.

Choosing Between Adjectives and Adverbs

Some words create problems because they have similar meanings or are commonly misused in daily conversations. For instance, confusing *bad* (the adjective) and *badly* (the adverb) is a common error. Here's an example:

> WRONG: I did really *bad* on the test, Dad.
>
> RIGHT: I did really *badly* on the test, Dad.
>
> WHY IT'S RIGHT: The adverb *badly* describes how I *did* (a verb).

Adjectives modify nouns or pronouns, and adverbs modify verbs, adjectives or other adverbs. So, let's look at some more of these commonly confused pairs.

Choosing between good and well

Logically, the adjective *good* should belong with the adverb *goodly*. Indeed, Edwardian gentlemen did use the word *goodly*, as in *goodly advice*, but you don't meet many Edwardian gentlemen these days, and today the word *goodly* has been replaced with the adverb *well*. However, when you're talking about your health, *well* is an adjective. Like this:

> What's that book you're reading? Is it any *good*? (*good* is an adjective describing *it*)

> Elton plays the piano *well*. (*well* is an adverb describing how Elton *plays* — *a verb*)

> I am *well*, thank you. (*well* is an adjective completing *I am* — *am* is a linking verb)

The second sentence is not *Elton plays the piano good*, because *good* is an adjective and what noun would it be describing as *good*? Elton? The piano? No, it's the way he *plays* that's *good*. In the third sentence, the sentence means *I am not sick*. Now look at this one:

> I'm *good*.

In this sentence, *good* is an adjective. Unfortunately, it's anybody's guess what the sentence really means. It could mean *I have the qualities of goodness (I've been nominated for Australian of the Year)*, or *I'm in a good mood*. But it's generally used to mean *I haven't finished the drink I've got, thanks*, or *I think that's a good idea, count me in*, or even *I don't need your help. Go away.* In formal writing, try to think of another word to replace *good* — a more interesting, accurate one that makes your meaning clear.

Choosing between real and really

Real and *really* work the same way as good and well (refer to preceding section). *Real* is an adjective (used to modify a noun) and *really* is an adverb (used to modify a verb, an adjective or another adverb — versatile little things).

> What's the *real* reason for your lateness?

Here *real* is an adjective modifying the noun *reason*. (What kind of reason? *Real* reason.)

> *Really* try to be honest.

Really is an adverb modifying the verb *try*. Try how? *Try really*.

> Try *really* hard to be honest.

In this example, *really* is an adverb modifying the adverb *hard*. Try (verb) how? Answer: *Try hard*. (So, *hard* is an adverb.) How hard? Answer: *Really hard*. *Really* is an adverb modifying the adverb *hard*. Easy, isn't it?!

> That's a *really* clever reason.

Really is an adverb here too, but it's not modifying a verb. It's modifying an adjective. What kind of reason (*reason* is the noun)? Answer: *Clever reason* (*clever* is the adjective). How clever? Answer: *Really clever*. So *really* is an adverb modifying the adjective *clever*. By now you should be really clever at this too.

Being Clear with Even, Almost and Only

A few modifying words — including *even*, *almost* and *only* — often end up in the wrong spots. If these words aren't placed correctly, your sentence may say something that you didn't intend.

Take a look at this example with *even*:

> Just before the premier of Sir Andrew's musical, the star of the show is struck by food poisoning. What will Sir Andrew do? Kylie has a suggestion, she shouts:
>
> POSSIBILITY 1: 'We can still go on! *Even Jason* knows the dances.'
>
> POSSIBILITY 2: 'We can still go on! Jason *even knows* the dances.'
>
> POSSIBILITY 3: 'We can still go on! Jason knows *even the dances.*'

These three statements look almost the same, but here's what each one means:

> POSSIBILITY 1: Kylie isn't worried. Anyone could save the day because the dances are simple. Jason is a total klutz, but *even Jason* knows the dances.

> POSSIBILITY 2: Kylie is excited because Jason's the obvious replacement — he knows everything, he *even knows* the dances.

> POSSIBILITY 3: Jason can handle the songs and already knows the dialogue. But can he manage the dances? To everyone's relief, Jason does indeed know *even the dances.*

Got it? Put *even* right in front of the words you want it to modify.

Almost is another tricky little modifier to place. Here's an example:

> Last night Sandy wrote for *almost an hour* and then went skating.

and

> Last night Sandy *almost wrote* for an hour and then went skating.

In the first sentence, Sandy wrote for 55 minutes and stopped. In the second, Sandy intended to write but, every time she sat down at the computer, she remembered that she hadn't watered the plants, called Midge, made a sandwich or whatever. After a wasted hour and without one word on the screen, she grabbed her skates and left.

Like the other words in this section, *only* changes the meaning of the sentence every time its position is altered. For example:

> *Only Bill* went to Iceland last summer. (No-one else went.)

> Bill *only went* to Iceland last summer. (He went, but he didn't do anything else.)

> Bill went *only to Iceland* last summer. (Just Iceland. He skipped Antarctica.)

> Bill went to Iceland *only last summer.* (Two possible meanings: either he didn't go three years ago or at any other time, but he did go last summer, or the word *only* means *just*, as in *recently*.)

When checking whether *only, even* and *almost* are in the right place in a sentence, play around with positioning to make sure your intended meaning is clear. Remember, they modify whatever follows them.

Understanding the Connection Between Which, That and the Comma

Confusion about the use of the pronouns *which* and *that* can lead your grammar checker to have a hissy fit. Traditionally, which one to choose depends on whether what follows the word is essential or extra information. *That* introduces information that the sentence can't do without — essential information that isn't set off from the rest of the sentence by commas. *Which* comes in front of non-essential information — extra information that isn't critical — and does require the use of commas.

Look at these:

> The piano that my mother gave me was the murder weapon. (*That* is part of the subject of the sentence. It's telling you the exact piano, of all the multitude of pianos I own, that was the murder weapon. It's essential information. The piano that my mother gave me — not any of my other pianos — was the murder weapon.)

> The piano, which my mother gave me, was the murder weapon. (Here, the information is given to you in a 'by the way' manner. It's not essential information and the commas indicate you could take it out and ignore it if you like. The piano was the murder weapon — and, by the way, my mother gave me that piano.)

Don't be frightened by your computer — it may underline every *which* that doesn't have a comma in front of it. This doesn't automatically mean that your sentence is wrong. It's a warning that you should check to see if your meaning is clear. By the way, this distinction in the use of *that* and *which* is dying, but you can avoid any confusion or ambiguity in your communication by understanding the difference between what's essential and what's not.

Creating Clear Comparisons

Is your knowledge of comparisons *more better* or *less worse*? English has two ways of creating comparisons, but you can't use them together and they're not interchangeable. In the following section, we cover how to use each correctly.

Controlling regular comparisons

Comparisons can be regular or irregular: the regular ones follow a pattern and the irregular ones like to assert their individuality. Pay close attention to the words in italics in each of the following sample sentences and see if you can work out the pattern for regular comparisons.

> Bill is *more outgoing* than his twin brother, but Ben is *thinner*.
>
> Bryce's *most recent* book is proving *more successful* than his *earlier* novel.
>
> Damian searched for the *least energy-efficient* sports car, believing that global warming is *less important* than having the *sexiest* image.

What did you notice? Some of the comparisons were expressed by adding -*er* or -*est*, and some were expressed by adding *more*, *most*, *less* or *least* to the quality that's being compared. How do you know which is appropriate? (Or, to use a comparison, how do you know which is *better*?) The dictionary is the final authority, and you should consult one if you're in doubt about a particular word. However, here are some general guidelines:

✔ Add -*er* and -*est* to most one-syllable adjectives.

✔ If the word already ends in the letter *e*, don't double the *e* by adding -*er* or -*est*. Just add -*r* or -*st*.

✔ Use –*er* and -*est* endings for words ending in –*ly* or for words of more than two syllables isn't usually appropriate.

Table 8-1 is a chart of some common descriptions, with both the -*er* and -*est* forms.

Table 8-1	Common Descriptions	
Description	*-er Form*	*-est Form*
bald	balder than a pumpkin	baldest of the accountants
dumb	dumber than a sea slug	dumbest of US presidents
friendly	friendlier than a labrador	friendliest person in the bar

Note that, when the last letter is *y*, often you must change the *y* to *i* before you tack on the ending.

Table 8-2 contains even more descriptions, this time with *more*, *less*, *most* and *least* added.

Table 8-2	Two-Word Descriptions	
Description	*More/Less Form*	*Most/Least Form*
magnificent	more magnificent than a work of art	most magnificent of all the sunsets
notorious	more notorious than a footballer	most notorious of the gangsters
rigid	less rigid than a grammarian	least rigid of the ticket inspectors

 Tables 8-1 and 8-2 give you a clue about another important comparison characteristic. Did you notice that the second column is always a comparison between *two* people or things? The addition of *-er* or *more* or *less* compares two things. In the last column of each table, the comparison is with a group with more than two members. When the group is larger than two, *-est* or *most* or *least* creates the comparison and identifies the extreme. To sum up the rules:

- ✔ Use *-er* or *more/less* when comparing only two things.

- ✔ Use *-est* or *most/least* when singling out the extreme in a group that's larger than two.

- ✔ Never combine two comparison methods, such as *-er* and *more*.

Mastering irregular comparisons

Whenever English grammar gives you a set of rules that make sense, you know it's time for the irregulars and exceptions to show up. Look at the following comparisons:

> Hank's constant teasing is *bad*, but Harry's compulsion to crack sick jokes is *worse*. However, Hetty's habit of always saying exactly what she thinks is the *worst* habit of all.

> Bruce has a *good* barbeque. Macca's is *better* than Carlso's, although it doesn't have a lid. But Johnno's six-burner with the built-in esky is the *best* of all the barbeques on the market.

Got the idea? Here's a list of the irregular comparisons:

- ✔ good, better, best
- ✔ bad, worse, worst
- ✔ well, better, best
- ✔ little, less, least
- ✔ many (or much), more, most.

These irregulars break the rules, but they're easy to remember. Three of the irregulars judge quality (*good, bad, well*) and two judge quantity (*little, many*).

Eradicating illogical comparisons

Is this section more unique than the previous one? No, definitely not. Why? Because nothing is *more unique*. The word *unique* means 'one of a kind'. Either something is one of a kind or it's not. Words like *unique* are *absolute*. Logically, you can't compare something that's unique with anything but itself.

The word *unique* is not unique. Several other words share its absolute quality. One is *perfect*: nothing is '*perfectest*'. Another is *dead*: *deader* is not more dead than dead! Other adjectives that absolutely fit into this category include *fatal, final, infinite, impossible, main, supreme, total, unanimous, universal* and *whole*. Here's an absolute at work:

> WRONG: Yasmin is *extremely perfect* when it comes to grammar.

> RIGHT: Yasmin is *perfect* when it comes to grammar.

> ALSO RIGHT: Yasmin is *nearly perfect* when it comes to grammar.

> WHY IT'S RIGHT: You can approach an absolute quality, comparing how close someone or something comes to the quality. Yasmin approaches perfection but doesn't achieve it.

Sometimes comparisons aren't logical because the comparison hasn't been finished. Consider the following sentence:

> Octavia screamed more chillingly.

Octavia screamed more chillingly . . . than what? Until you finish the sentence, your readers are left with as many possibilities as they can imagine. Bottom line: don't stop explaining your comparison until you get your point across. Let's fix that illogical sample sentence:

> Octavia screamed more chillingly than the cat did the day James drove over its tail.

Storytelling in Past or Present Tense

Wiping her three eyes, the alien *told* us her story. The bottom level of her ship *caught* fire and one computer *exploded*. Flames *destroyed* all the sleeping quarters. When she *requested* clearance to berth, the controllers *thought* she *said* Earth, and *beamed* her into our backyard.

In the story, the verbs (in italics) are all in the *past tense* — the action of the verb is complete. But people also talk about past events in the *present tense* — the action of the verb happens now. Sporting commentators do it all the time. Novels do it. You probably do it when you talk to friends. But you need to be careful about mixing your tenses. Read on.

Choosing past or present tense

When storytelling, either present or past tense is acceptable. Using the present tense can add an extra dose of drama to a story by making it sound more immediate (which is why jokes are told in present tense). Readers and listeners tend to notice present tense. Here's a present tense tale with the verbs in italics:

> The day *passes* like any other until a massive magpie *swoops* out of nowhere and *grabs* Bert's favourite toupee. Bert *feels* the cold air *slap* his shiny head. He *calls* to Patty for help but she *ignores* him and *continues* the time-consuming job of sticking her split-ends back together.

Using the past tense to recount a tale is more conventional. Reporters use past tense. Here is the past tense version of the same paragraph, with the verbs in italics:

> The day *passed* like any other until a massive magpie *swooped* out of nowhere and *grabbed* Bert's favourite toupee. Bert *felt* the cold air *slap* his shiny head. He *called* to Patty for help but she *ignored* him and *continued* the time-consuming job of sticking her split-ends back together.

Although past tense is more familiar to readers and listeners, many popular novels are written in present tense because the reader needs to be involved as if the action is happening while they read (as in Suzanne Collins's *The Hunger Games*, for example). To choose between past and present, decide which best suits your story, and then stick with it.

Use the present tense when you discuss a novel, film or work of art. Once it's finished, a piece of art is constant. It may have been created in the past, but it has a permanent form.

Mixing tenses

You can make a statement about something that always happens (someone's custom or habit) using the present tense. And if you combine that statement with a story about events that have finished, the story may begin in the present tense and move to the past tense:

> George *works* at a market garden every Saturday morning. Before he *goes*, he *asks* Mabel what vegetables she *wants*. He never *forgets* the list and *brings* back exactly what she *requests*.

Until this point in the story, all the verbs are in the present tense because the story tells of George's habits. The same events happen every Saturday. In the next sentence, however, the story switches to the past tense because it examines one unusual day in the past.

> Last Saturday, Mabel *knew* that something had *upset* George because he *brought* her a cabbage and some potatoes, but she'd *asked* for a cauliflower and some carrots. Nothing was *said* as they *ate* lunch, but over

a cup of tea afterwards, George *saw* the confusion in Mabel's eyes and *knew* she was *worried*.

You're also allowed to slip the present tense in with the past tense if the thing you're talking about is still happening (even if it isn't a statement about a habit). For example:

'That *was* Bryce,' *said* my mother. 'He *says* that his latest book *is* number one in the bestseller list.' (It hasn't stopped being number one since she put the phone down, and Bryce is still telling anyone who'll listen.)

Mixing tenses when you're talking about past events is *not* acceptable.

Choosing between done and did

The word *done* is never a verb all by itself. A true party animal, this verb form only exists as part of a verb group. In grammarspeak, *done* is the past participle of the verb *to do* and participles never function as main verbs in sentences. Here are some examples:

WRONG: He done all he could, but Sylvia was still not happy.

RIGHT: He had done all he could, but Sylvia was still not happy. (*had* is the main verb)

WRONG: She done him a favour.

RIGHT: She did him a favour. (*did* is the past tense of the verb *to do*)

You may blame the fact that so many people create sentences like *He done all he could* on one of the many joys of English grammar: some past participles look exactly the same as the plain past tense. Consider the verb *to wait*:

PLAIN PAST TENSE VERB: I *waited* 20 years.

PAST PARTICIPLE IN VERB GROUP: I *have waited* 20 years.

WHY ENGLISH DOES THIS: Your guess is as good as anyone else's.

You may use verbs like *waited* alone or in a verb group because the same word may be both a past tense verb and a past participle. Verbs that work this way are called *regular verbs*. (Refer to Chapter 2 for more about verbs.) You may not use *done* by itself as a verb, however, because it's not the past tense of *to do*. The past tense of *to do* is *did*. Verbs with different words for the past participle and the past tense are called *irregular verbs*.

Using lie, lay, laid, lain

Whoever invented the verbs *lie* and *lay* had an evil sense of humour. *Lie* means 'not to tell the truth'. *Lie* also means 'to get yourself horizontal'. *Lay* means 'to put something down, to place something'. (The slang version of *lay* seems to be used as a combination of all those meanings but let's not go there.) Here's a clean, safe example:

> Nanna *lies* down for an hour after lunch. Before she *lies* down, she *lays* a blanket on the couch.

So far, this topic isn't too complicated. The problem — and the truly evil part — comes in the past tense. The past tense of *lie* (to rest, to recline, to remain) is *lay*. The past tense of *lay* (to put or place) is *laid*. Check out this example:

> Nanna *lay* down for an hour after lunch yesterday. As usual, she *laid* a blanket on the couch.

By now you're probably thinking, but what about the chooks? They *lay*, and they sure as eggs aren't doing it in the past tense. They *lay* right here and now. And they're not horizontal either! Well, it's the same verb we used when Nanna *lay* the rug down. The chooks 'put something down' — eggs. This is another rule about the verb *lay* (to place). It always takes an object. Something (the object — see Chapter 3 for a full explanation of objects) has to be put down. And you can remember that easily because chooks *lay* objects — eggs are objects, right? So:

> Our chooks *lay* their eggs in the wash basket.

> We *lay* the foundations for good grammar at your feet.

One more complication. When you add *has*, *had* or *have* to the verb *lay* (to put or place), you say *has laid*, *had laid*, *have laid*. When you add *has*, *had* or *have* to the verb *lie* (to rest, to recline, to remain), the correct form is *has lain*, *had lain*, *have lain*. In other words:

> Nanna *has lain* down for an hour after lunch every day of her married life. For the last millennium, she *has laid* a blanket on the couch first.

To recap, that's *lie*, *lay*, *have lain*, but *lay*, *laid*, *have laid*. (If you're feeling uncomfortable with *lain*, you can do what most people do and avoid *has lain* and *had lain* by using *has been lying* and *had been lying*. This will get you out of most tricky situations — and we haven't lied to you!) So after all that, you probably reckon you need a good lie down.

Matching Up Two-Part Conjunctions

Most joining words fly solo. They're free to act singularly — *and*, *but*, *nor*, *or*, *because*, *although*, *since* and so on. Some joining words, however, come in pairs. (In grammarspeak, two-part conjunctions are called *correlative conjunctions* or *correlatives*.) Here are some of the most frequently used correlative conjunctions:

- ✔ not only ... but also
- ✔ either ... or
- ✔ neither ... nor
- ✔ whether ... or
- ✔ both ... and.

Sometimes words that can form correlative conjunctions show up in sentences without their partners. No problem. Sometimes they show up and don't act as conjunctions. Again, no problem. When problems can occur is when they're acting in tandem as two-part conjunctions. If you don't handle them properly, your computer may identify this problem with its warning squiggly line. Here's the rule: whatever fills in the blanks after these pairs of conjunctions must match. The conjunctions have partners, and so do the things they join. You may join two nouns, two sentences, two prepositional phrases — two whatevers, as long as each element is equal. We grammarphiles call this *parallel construction*. If you don't join two equal things, the construction won't be parallel. So, to revise the error, make the things that you join match. Revise the sentence so that they mirror each other.

Look at these examples of correlative conjunctions:

Ravi wanted *not only* to visit Port Douglas *but also* he hoped to learn to windsurf. (Error: *to visit* doesn't match with *he hoped to learn*.)

Ravi wanted *not only* to visit Port Douglas *but also* to learn to windsurf. (Correct revision: *to learn* mirrors *to visit*.)

Either you break the news of the engagement to Molly *or* not. (Error: *you* doesn't match *not*.)

Either you break the news of the engagement to Molly *or* you do not. (Correct revision: *you* is now mirrored by itself after each part of the conjunction pair.)

Ending the Problem with 1 or Me

A grammar disaster of near-tsunami-sized proportion results from the way prepositions interact with pronouns. A *pronoun* is a word that substitutes for a noun. Okay, so the problem isn't really that immense, but it's pretty common, and it's also pretty easy to avoid. Only some pronouns are allowed to act as objects of prepositions; they're specifically called *object pronouns*. (Refer to Chapter 4 for details on pronoun rules.) Use the wrong pronoun — one that's not an object pronoun — and you'll be swept up in the tidal wave of error-makers.

The pronouns you can safely use as objects of the preposition are *me*, *you*, *him*, *her*, *it*, *us*, *them*, *whom* and *whomever*. Take a look at these sentences:

I have a plan, but please keep this between *you* and *me*. (*You* and *me* are the objects of the preposition *between*.)

Without *them*, the sky will surely fall. (*Them* is the object of the preposition *without*.)

The email contains some comments about *us*. (*Us* is the object of the preposition *about*.)

The most common dilemma in the use of pronouns is whether to use the prepositional phrase *between you and I* or *between you and me*. Answer: The correct expression is *between you and me* because *I* is a *subject pronoun*, so it can't be used as the object of anything, including prepositions.

 Most of the tough pronoun choices come when the sentence has more than one object of the preposition. Your ear for grammar will probably tell you the correct pronoun when the sentence has a single pronoun object. You probably wouldn't say *according to she* because it sounds funny (to use a technical explanation).

If the sentence has more than one object of the preposition, try this rule of thumb. Take your thumb and cover one of the objects. Say the sentence. Does it sound right? Try it with this sentence:

> Jarvis popped the cork for Kelsey and I/me.

Which one is correct? Take your thumb and cover the first object. Say the sentence. Does it sound right?

> Jarvis popped the cork for Kelsey.

So far, so good. No problem with the sound of that. Now put your thumb over the first possibility for the second object and read the sentence again.

> Jarvis popped the cork for I.

Yuk. That can't be right. Do you hear the problem? Make the change:

> Jarvis popped the cork for me.

That's better. Now put the two back together:

> Jarvis popped the cork for Kelsey and me.

This method is not foolproof, but you have a good chance of getting a clue to the correct pronoun choices if you check the objects one by one.

Editing Out Empty Subjects: Its, Here and There

Someone comes up to you and says, 'Here is a million dollars.' What's the first question that comes into your mind? Obviously, with your burning interest in grammar, it's 'What's the subject of that sentence?' Well, try to answer that question in the usual way:

> Here is a million dollars.

1. **Ask yourself the questions: What's happening? What is?**

   Answer: *Is*.

2. **Ask yourself the questions: Who *is*? What *is*?**

   Answer: *?*

Did you say *here* is? But *here* can't be a subject (it isn't a noun or a pronoun — and to be a legal subject, it must be a noun equivalent). Neither can *there*. *Here* and *there* are empty subjects or fakers. Although they're in the place usually occupied by the subject, *here* and *there* don't decide the form of the verb. You don't know whether to say *is* or *are* until you get to the real subject (which is, of course, what the verb agrees with — refer to Chapter 2 for more information). Fill in the gaps in each of these sentences with *is* or *are* to see what the subject really is:

> Here ... a frog for you to put in Bobo's bed.

It has to be *Here is a frog*; the verb agrees with *frog*, so that's the real subject (a frog is here for you to put in Bobo's bed). Now try this one:

> There ... four tickets under the fridge magnet.

There are four tickets, so *tickets* is the real subject (four tickets are there under the fridge magnet). Although they sometimes try to fake it as nouns, *here* and *there* are actually adverbs. *Adverbs* modify verbs, adjectives and other adverbs. They're busy little words. (For more on adverbs, refer to Chapter 5.)

The moral of this story is: avoid *here* and *there* when searching for the subject of a sentence. And always be sure that the verb agrees with the real subject. Better still, revise your sentence to edit out the empty subject and you'll have to choose a more interesting active verb instead of relying on some bland part of the verb *to be*. The preceding sample sentences could be:

> Hide this frog in Bobo's bed.

> Four tickets await under the fridge magnet.

Another little word that functions as an empty subject is the pronoun *it*. Legally, of course, *it* can serve as a real subject, but consider this sentence:

> It's a glorious day.

What *is*? Answer: *It is*. But which noun is the pronoun *it* standing in for? The following sentences illuminate the real subject:

> Today is glorious.

> The weather is glorious today.

Each of these sentences is more specific than the version with the empty subject. So remember, to communicate clearly, your sentence must have a clear subject–verb pair. Edit your work to eliminate empty subjects and your readers will thank you.

Ending a Sentence with a Preposition

In the midst of truly earth-shattering events, some people actually worry about whether or not ending a sentence with a preposition is acceptable, and their justification is based on the logic that a word called a *preposition* must *pre*-position something. 'By definition,' they exclaim as they point their accusing fingers at the offending word, 'a preposition must come in front of a noun or noun equivalent. Thus, it is not acceptable for the last word of a sentence to be a preposition.' Well, let's test their theory:

> Tell me what you are thinking *about*.

> Tell me *about* what you are thinking.

Guess what? Both sentences are acceptable. Those finger-wavers would like you to believe that only sentence two is correct.

Well, they're wrong. And here's why. Sometimes, a preposition acts as an additional word to make a two-part verb. When this happens, the preposition becomes part of a verb group and is not acting as a preposition at all. In the preceding sample sentence, the preposition *about* is more closely related to the verb group *are thinking* than it is to any of the noun equivalents in the sentence. A difference in meaning exists between *to think about* (to consider) and *to think* (to believe). Hence, you have no logical reason not to finish the sentence with the offending word, because it's part of a compound verb or verb group, and no law prevents the use of verbs at the end of a sentence, even in Fingerpointerville.

So, if ever you encounter one of the aforementioned worriers, make either of these suggestions:

> Why don't you relax and *turn* your mental grammar checker *off?*

> Why don't you relax and *turn off* your mental grammar checker?

Explain to these rule-lovers that ending a sentence with a preposition is perfectly acceptable, because sometimes it just sounds like a preposition.

Chapter 9

Reporting Speech and Quoting Others

⁘ ⁘

In This Chapter

▶ Defining a *quotation*

▶ Dealing with block quotes

▶ Learning to use ellipses and brackets in quotes

▶ Understanding how to present titles

▶ Relaying conversations and thoughts

▶ Considering 'scare quotes' to highlight words and phrases

⁘ ⁘

*P*unctuation is often a matter of style rather than grammar. In this chapter, we tell you how to handle quotations and punctuate speech in the simplest way acceptable here in the Land of Oz. We also explain how to use 'scare quotes' correctly in your writing (that's what you call those quotation marks people make in the air with their fingers).

Quoting Someone Else

A *quotation* is a repetition of someone else's written or spoken words — just one word or a whole statement or passage. You see quotations in almost all forms of writing.

When a quotation consists of a few words but not a complete sentence, you can put these words inside the very appropriately named *quotation marks* in a sentence of your own. If you're quoting whole sentences, it's a bit more complicated. Here are the rules:

- ✔ Put a short quotation of complete sentences (up to about three lines) inside quotation marks within the text of whatever you are writing.

- ✔ Indent and single-space a longer quotation, with space above and below it, so that it looks like a separate block of print. Such quotations are called *displayed* quotations or *block* quotes.

- ✔ Use the block quote format to indicate the lines of a poem when writing about poetry.

Here's an example of a *block quote* from an imaginary book:

> Witherby, in his paper 'Why Homework Is Useless', makes the following point:
>
> > A study of 1,000 students reveals that those who have no time to rest are not as efficient as those who do. Teens surveyed all indicated that sleeping is more valuable than homework, as is listening to music, talking with friends on the phone or computer and watching television.

Quote or *quotation*? Strictly speaking, *quote* is what you do (in other words, it's the verb *to quote*), and a *quotation* is the text you're quoting (thus a noun — so you *quote* a *quotation*). Technically, the punctuation marks you use to indicate the quotation are called *quotation marks*. In conversational English, *quote* and *quotation* have long been interchangeable. The difference between the two words is being lost; now, you'll find *quote marks* used even in some formal grammar references.

Punctuating Block Quotations

The simplest way to punctuate a block quotation is to introduce each one with a colon (as we have in the preceding section). You're allowed to do this whether the text before the quotation is a complete sentence or not.

Note that we didn't use any quotation marks around the example in the preceding section. That's because the space around the quotation shows that you're quoting, so quotation marks are unnecessary.

When a quotation is not set as a block, you can't leave the quotation marks out because you need to show where the words you're quoting begin and end:

> Witherby notes that 'Teens surveyed all indicated that sleeping is more valuable than homework'.

You need to note three important things here. One is the capital *T* in the middle of the sentence. It's necessary because a capital letter is used at the start of the quotation. Another is the absence of a colon. A colon isn't needed when you include someone else's words in your sentence. And, finally, the full stop is outside the quotation marks. The words quoted come from inside one of Witherby's sentences, not at the end with a full stop. So, the full stop belongs at the conclusion of the whole sentence.

Sometimes, you may not want or need to use every word in a quotation. Look at this:

> Witherby goes on to say that 'When 1,000 teens were surveyed, they all indicated that ... listening to music ... and watching television were more valuable than schoolwork.'

For our purpose, some words aren't relevant, so we've put three dots to show we've left something out. The dots tell our readers that we've done this, and they can check the original text if they want to see what we've left out. (These little dots are called *ellipses* or *ellipsis points*. Don't change the channel. You can find more information on ellipses in the next section.)

The other important thing about this last example is that we don't seem to have a full stop for our own sentence. That's because we don't need two full stops. If what you're quoting concludes with a full stop, you have to make a choice. These are both correct:

> He goes on to say that 'Teens ... indicated that sleeping is more valuable than homework, as is listening to music, talking with friends ... and watching television.' (We've used Professor Witherby's full stop and let it end our sentence as well.)

> He goes on to say that 'Teens ... indicated that sleeping is more valuable than homework, as is listening to music, talking with friends ... and watching television'. (We've left out the professor's full stop — ending the quotation just one tiny dot too early — and used our own full stop to end the whole sentence.)

Joining the Dots with Ellipses

When you're quoting someone else's words, you can't leave bits out without saying so. It's just plain rude! So place three dots (and only three dots — never five or six or more) wherever you've left out words from the original. As mentioned in the preceding section, the dots are called *ellipses*. (One set is an *ellipsis*.)

If you delete the end of a sentence, don't use four dots. Omit the full stop. You can, however, add an exclamation mark or question mark before or after an ellipsis. You'll see ellipses with and without spaces around them. Aussie style is to put a space before and after an ellipsis.

Have a look at Ingrid's description of what she did last night, as written in her diary. The parts that she'll leave out when she explains to her teacher why she hasn't done her homework are in italics:

> I sat down at the computer last night to write the essay. I truly love writing essays, *not,* and I certainly want to do well in this class *if I can get good grades without doing a stitch of work.* I began to write shortly before eight o'clock, but *the phone rang almost immediately. I spoke with my friends for no more than three hours. Then my mother asked me if I wanted a snack. I said yes. I ate two or three large pizzas and settled down at the computer. Then* my stomach hurt, and I was very tired. I had to go to bed. I'll do the essay tonight.

And here's the edited version, punctuated with ellipses:

> I sat down at the computer last night to write the essay. I truly love writing essays ... and I certainly want to do well in this class ... I began to write shortly before eight o'clock, but ... my stomach hurt, and I was very tired. I had to go to bed. I'll do the essay tonight.

All the ellipses have three dots with a space either side ... The third ellipsis covers a multitude of sins — whole sentences missing plus a bit of a sentence. Using an ellipsis connects the remaining text on both sides of the deleted text so it is read as if it were a connected sentence.

By omitting some of the information, Ingrid's being dishonest and you shouldn't follow her example! One of the most important issues in writing is credibility. If you change the meaning of what you're quoting by leaving out crucial details, your readers will figure this out eventually, and then they won't trust anything you say. (Also, your teacher may fail you.) Check the passage you're quoting before and after you've cut it. Do both convey the same message? If not, don't cut it (or cut differently).

You can also use ellipses to show hesitation or indecision, particularly in dialogue:

> I don't know what to do about that bill! It's already overdue ... I shouldn't have ... I just don't have ... What am I going to do?

Beware: using ellipses in this way can get really annoying really quickly. Don't overdo it.

Putting Brackets within Quotations

You're probably familiar with round brackets, which are called *parentheses* (such as shown here). But, when you're quoting something and adding words of your own in the middle of the quotation, you use *square brackets* to let the reader know that these words weren't part of the original. For example, if we were reporting that Charlotte had written in her essay about Einstein that the 20th century (as we know it) began with the five papers he wrote in 1905, we'd do it like this:

> Charlotte wrote in her essay that 'the 20th century (as we know it) began with the five papers that he [Einstein] wrote in 1905'.

Charlotte wrote *(as we know it)*, including the parentheses, but she didn't write the word *Einstein*; she wrote *he*. We had to add *[Einstein]* so that you'd know who she was talking about.

The word most commonly added to quotations using square brackets in this way is *sic*. This is Latin for *thus* (or *Don't blame us for this mistake — it's in the original*). For example:

> Lucinda wrote in her history essay that 'Mary Queen of Scots went to her cousin Elizabeth for refuse [*sic*]'.

Lucinda meant *refuge*, but that's not what she wrote. We put the *[sic]* in so that you'd know it was Lucinda's mistake, not a spelling mistake in *English Grammar Essentials For Dummies*. These brackets are always square, and *sic* is in italics to show that it isn't an English word.

Sometimes, putting words inside round brackets (*parentheses*) is useful. Like we've just done here. Doing so separates those words from the rest of the sentence to give them a specific emphasis. As brackets come in pairs, it's a good idea to check what you've written to make sure both halves of the pair are there when you use brackets. (If you need to put brackets inside brackets, use square brackets [also just called *brackets*] for the inside pair.) Just like the preceding sentence.

The rules for adding a full stop with brackets (round or square) are clear. A full stop belongs to the sentence, not to the words in brackets. The full stop only goes inside the brackets if the whole sentence is inside the brackets. Look at this example:

> WRONG: Susie loves Christmas, especially now that Max is old enough to enjoy it. (She particularly misses her mother at Christmas, though).

> RIGHT: Susie loves Christmas, especially now that Max is old enough to enjoy it. (She particularly misses her mother at Christmas, though.)

And one more rule: you should never put a comma *before* an opening bracket. Look at this sentence:

> WRONG: All year round, but especially in the summer, (when the nights are hot), Raj suffers from insomnia.

> ALSO WRONG: All year round, but especially in the summer, (when the nights are hot) Raj suffers from insomnia.

> RIGHT: All year round, but especially in the summer (when the nights are hot), Raj suffers from insomnia.

> EVEN BETTER: All year round, but especially in the summer when the nights are hot, Raj suffers from insomnia. (Don't overuse brackets.)

Recording Titles

Sometimes in your writing, you may need to record the name of a magazine, the headline of a newspaper article, the title of a song or film and so on. It's important to show the reader which words are part of the title, so they need to be separated from the text in some way. You have two ways to do this:

1. **Put the title in quotation marks.** This is the usual way to indicate titles of smaller works or parts of a whole.

2. **Set the title off from the rest of the writing with italics.** Titles of larger works or complete works are treated in this way.

Use quotation marks for the titles of

- ✓ chapters
- ✓ individual episodes of a television series
- ✓ magazine and newspaper articles
- ✓ poems
- ✓ short stories and essays
- ✓ songs.

Use italics for the titles of

- ✓ books and collections of poetry, stories and essays
- ✓ magazines and newspapers
- ✓ recorded works of art such as musical albums and DVDs
- ✓ television programs, plays and films.

Also use italics for the names of specific paintings and sculptural works, ships, aircraft, trains and other vehicles.

Here are some examples of quotation marks and italics for titles:

- ✓ 'A thousand dodgy deductions' (a newspaper article) in *Revenue News* (a newspaper)
- ✓ 'Ode to the tax man' (a poem) in *Economic E-coli* (an anthology of poetry)
- ✓ 'The self-assessment blues' (a song title) on *Me and My Taxes* (an album containing many songs)

> ✔ 'On the art of negative gearing' (an essay) in *Getting Rich and Staying Rich* (a magazine)
>
> ✔ 'Small business expenses' (an individual episode) on *The World of Taxation* (a television series).

 You may be wondering which letters you should capitalise in a title. A useful general rule is that anything that's in italics can have a capital letter on every important word, including the first and last word, important or not. Anything in quotation marks usually has only one capital letter, at the start of the title. (For more information on capitalisation, refer to Chapter 7.)

Writing Conversation: Quotation Marks

If you're a fiction writer and/or reader, or intend to write a memoir, knowing the way to punctuate speech is important. Quite a few rules are involved and, if you read things that have been published in the US or the UK, you'll find different styles are used in each country. So we're going to give you the easiest and most consistent Aussie way, and, in true-blue style, the others can go jump!

If you learned this kind of punctuation at primary school, you may have called them talking marks. You'll find them referred to as inverted commas, quotation marks or the shortened form of the latter, quotes.

First, you need to be clear about the difference between when the exact words spoken are recorded (direct speech) and when they're just reported (indirect speech).

Indicating indirect speech

Indirect speech tells you about a conversation, but it doesn't give people's exact words. It's a report of their ideas, but not a record of the words actually spoken or written, and it needn't use any of their own words. The rules for punctuating indirect speech are the same as the rules for text in general:

> Mrs Robinson, who lives next door to the accused, spoke to our reporter after the arrest. She said she is shocked by recent events, and expressed her sympathy for the

victim of the alleged crime. Mrs Robinson claims that the whole grammar-loving community has been greatly upset by the tawdry nature of Ms Stakes's secret life.

Dealing with direct speech

The following are examples of *direct speech*:

'It'll be lonely for you when Natasha moves interstate.'

'Yes, I expect it will.'

'But it'll be a relief knowing that she's not going to blow something up with one of her experiments.'

'That's true. I always feel safer when she's in one of her non-nuclear phases.'

We're quoting the speakers' exact words. You need to notice three important things about these examples.

The first thing is that single quotation marks are used. The argument about single or double is one of style. Newspaper style generally uses doubles, whereas most novels and magazines use singles. Who's right? Or maybe the question should be 'Who's least wrong?' The trend in Australian style is to minimise punctuation (to use the minimum amount necessary). So, single quotation marks are preferred in Australia. (The KISS principle applies to punctuation as to so many other aspects of life — Keep It Simple Stupid!)

The second thing you need to notice is that in direct speech, such as the examples at the start of this section, the end punctuation of the words spoken always (*always*) goes *inside* the quotation marks. It could be a full stop, an exclamation mark or a question mark, but put it inside the quotation marks. Like this:

'What will you do when Natasha's gone?'

'I'll be able to eat chips in the bath undisturbed!'

The question mark and exclamation mark are helpful in telling you how the speakers are saying the words. That seems simple enough. ***Note:*** An *always* rule is a bonus in a grammar filled with exceptions and unusual cases.

Now for the third thing you need to notice. In each of the example sentences, the direct speech forms the entire sentence. This is not always the case with direct speech. The following section looks at what happens when other words are added.

Being formal with carrier expressions

Sometimes other words are used to form a sentence that contains direct speech. Like this:

> 'Might I ask your reasons?' he growled.

> I replied from the other side of his vast desk, 'Well, sir, I just thought it was a good idea'.

> 'That', he said, 'was clearly not your best thought'.

An expression in a sentence that carries a piece of direct speech is called (... drum roll ... gasp of expectation ...) a *carrier expression*. Yep, you can breathe easy. You're not going to burst any brain cells trying to remember that clever little tag. The bit that might cause just the tiniest bit of brain strain, however, comes when we talk about punctuating carrier expressions. According to acceptable Australian style for formal writing, especially non-fiction writing, when the direct speech is attached to a carrier expression, the full stop comes at the end of the complete sentence — which means putting the full stop outside the quotation marks, as in the preceding sample conversation. (For more information on formal language, refer to Chapter 1.)

Sorry, but more rule-related brain injury is yet to come. Look at these sentences:

> She screamed, 'I don't believe you!'

> Politely he enquired, 'Would you believe me?'

If you apply the carrier expression rule, each of the preceding sample sentences would have a full stop at the end of it because the direct speech is attached to a carrier expression. That would give you one punctuation point at the end of the quotation (an exclamation mark or a question mark) and another at the end of the entire sentence (a full stop). But putting two separate punctuation marks at the end of one sentence would be punctuation maximisation — the opposite of minimisation and of the KISS principle. So, when two types of end punctuation could occur together, choose the stronger one. Exclamation marks and question marks are stronger than full stops. Put the exclamation mark or question mark inside the quotation mark and omit the full stop at the end of the expression.

To recap this style for formal English, if the entire sentence is a piece of direct speech, put the end punctuation inside the quotation marks. If the direct speech is attached to a carrier expression and is an ordinary statement, put the final punctuation at the very end of the entire expression. If the direct speech ends the sentence and is a question or an exclamation, put the end punctuation inside the quotation mark.

 Now for the good news. In Australian newspapers (which are meant to be non-fiction), informal writing and in fiction, these rules about end punctuation with carrier expressions are rarely applied. All the end punctuation, no matter whether the direct speech is a statement, a question or an exclamation, goes inside the final quotation marks. Phew! So, unless you're writing something formal — such as a report, university assignment or submission for an academic journal — you can ignore the carrier expression rule and opt for the easier 'always' rule. Always put the end punctuation inside the closing quotation marks whether you're writing a carrier expression or not — like we do in this book.

Putting the speaker first

This and the following two sections look at different ways of putting the direct speech into a carrier sentence, starting with what happens when you put speakers before their words. And remember, we're applying the 'always' rule here (refer to preceding section for more).

> Cynthia moaned, 'Nobody ever misses me.'
>
> Natasha smiled, 'Well, we might if you ever went anywhere!'

Note that we've put a comma before the opening quotation mark and that the direct speech begins with a capital letter. (Newspapers generally use a colon instead of a comma to introduce direct speech, and some writers prefer a colon if the speech is long, but you don't have to bother. Stick to an 'always' rule and you can't go wrong.)

Putting the speaker last

If you put the information about who's speaking after the speech, you move the full stop to the end of your whole sentence (which will, of course, now be outside the quotes) and replace it with some other punctuation: a comma, question mark or exclamation mark. Everything else remains unchanged.

> 'Yes,' said her flatmate without looking up from his newspaper.

> 'Yes?' queried her flatmate without looking up from his newspaper.

> 'Yes!' agreed her flatmate without looking up from his newspaper.

Note especially that no capital letter is used after the comma (as you'd expect), but a capital letter isn't used after the question mark or exclamation mark either. You may think this is odd. Exclamation marks and question marks end sentences, so there should be a capital letter, right? Wrong! This is just one of the peculiarities of the rules with speech. These punctuation marks are regarded as indicating tone of voice rather than the end of the sentence (which comes where the full stop is).

Putting the speaker in the middle

Sometimes the information about who is speaking lands in the middle of a sentence:

> 'It's a great relief,' Chandra said, 'that I don't have to convince Cynthia to stay tonight.'

In this sentence, the speech is interrupted to tell you who's speaking. Right there in the middle, we've added

> , Chandra said,

Here are the rules for interruptions to sentences.

Rule 1: Nothing about the original speech changes. A capital letter isn't used at the start of the second half. But two more quotation marks must be used so that you still know which words are being spoken and which are just telling you who's speaking.

Rule 2: The interruption has to have a pair of commas, and the second comma goes at the end of the interruption.

Rule 3: The first comma always goes *inside* the quotation marks as though it's part of the first half of the speech.

Note that, in the interrupted quotations in this section, the quoted material adds up to only one sentence even though it's written in two separate parts.

Take care when writing direct speech that you don't create a run-on sentence. A *run-on sentence* is actually two sentences that have been stuck together (that is, *run* together) with nothing legal to join them. (For more information on run-on sentences, see Chapter 12.) Even in direct speech you must obey the rules about joining sentences or both your computer and your reader could become confused. Check out these examples:

> WRONG: 'I don't understand why you're so soft on Damian,' complained Ellie, 'he's so unreliable.'

> RIGHT: 'I don't understand why you're so soft on Damian,' complained Ellie. 'He's so unreliable.'

The spoken material forms two complete sentences:

> SENTENCE 1: I don't understand why you're so soft on Damian.

> SENTENCE 2: He's so unreliable.

Because the spoken material forms two complete sentences, you must write two separate sentences. If you cram this quoted material into one sentence, you create a run-on sentence error.

To check for a run-on sentence, remove the information about who's speaking and check the spoken material. What's left? Enough for half a sentence? That's okay. A speech doesn't need to express a complete thought. Enough material for one sentence? Also okay. Enough material for two sentences? Not okay, unless you write two sentences.

Including speech within speech

People don't just talk *to* each other; they also talk *about* each other. They recount stories and repeat what so-and-so said about such-and-such — like this.

> Bill said, 'Mildred had the nerve to say my galahs are upsetting her snakes!'

Well, that's okay, but what if Bill wants to include Mildred's exact words? You need some more quotation marks:

> Bill said, 'Mildred had the nerve to say "Your galahs are upsetting my snakes!"'

A sentence like this has to be sorted out. The first rule is that, as you're using single quotation marks to start with, you use double quotes for the inner speech.

Commas and end punctuation follow the same general rules in both double and single quotations. But, when you're quoting a complete sentence (inside another piece of direct speech), you should only put the appropriate end punctuation at the end of the sentence you're quoting. Look at the sentence in layers, working from the inside out, and then get rid of any duplicated end punctuation.

Asking questions within questions

If a sentence includes quoted words and the whole sentence is a question but the quoted words aren't, the question mark goes outside the quote marks. (Imagine giving both parts their punctuation and then deciding which to keep. A question mark or exclamation mark is more informative than a full stop, so it's stronger. That's the one to keep.)

> STEP 1 (WRONG): Did I hear that right? Did you just say, 'I don't like chocolate.'?
>
> STEP 2 (LOSE THE FULL STOP): Did I hear that right? Did you just say, 'I don't like chocolate'?
>
> STEP 1 (WRONG): Yes. I said, 'I don't like chocolate.'!
>
> STEP 2 (LOSE THE FULL STOP): Yes. I said, 'I don't like chocolate'!

But, for those rare occasions when both the quoted words and the sentence are questions or exclamations, put the question mark or exclamation mark inside the quotation marks. (Imagine giving both their punctuation to start with and then keeping one. One placed outside the quotes stands for the whole sentence only, as in the preceding examples. But one placed inside does double duty for both — just as a full stop in speech always does. So that's the one you keep.) Here's an example:

> STEP 1 (WRONG): Did Damian really ask Alice, 'Why do you eat rabbit food?'?

STEP 2 (LOSE THE SPARE OUTSIDE QUESTION MARK. RIGHT): Did Damian really ask Alice, 'Why do you eat rabbit food?'

STEP 1 (WRONG): Yes! And, when she tried to defend her choice to be a vegetarian, he said, 'Oh, get a life!'!

STEP 2 (LOSE THE SPARE OUTSIDE EXCLAMATION MARK. RIGHT): Yes! And, when she tried to defend her choice to be a vegetarian, he said, 'Oh, get a life!'

Showing a change of speaker

In a conversation (as opposed to an earbashing), people take turns speaking. Take a look at this extremely mature discussion:

'You sat on my tuna sandwich,' Lucinda said.

'No, I didn't,' Martin said.

'Yes, you did,' Lucinda said.

'Did not!' Martin said.

'Did too!' Lucinda said.

Note that every time the speaker changes, we start a new paragraph, which makes the conversation easy to follow; the reader always knows who's talking.

Here's another version of the tuna fight:

'You sat on my tuna sandwich,' Lucinda said.

'No, I didn't,' Martin replied.

'Yes, you did.'

'Did not!'

'Did too!'

Sounds better, doesn't it? You can figure out who's speaking because of the paragraph breaks, so we can leave out a lot of boring repeated information about who's speaking.

So the rule is this: every change of speaker is signalled by a new paragraph.

You may have read some novels in which the author and editor have decided to break away from the traditional rules for punctuating direct speech and to keep the punctuation so clean and simple that they use no quotation marks at all. (James Joyce, as far back as 1914, called quotation marks 'perverted commas'.) Starting a new line for a new speaker is critical to this style, because it's often the only clue readers get that somebody is speaking. We're not suggesting you don't use quotation marks just yet. But, if you follow all the advice in this chapter, you'll be able to have a deep and meaningful discussion with your publisher about postmodern fashion in quotation marks when you're working out the details of your first book deal!

A new paragraph signals each speaker change, no matter how short the speeches. This rule applies even if the argument deteriorates into single-word statements such as

> 'Yes!'
>
> 'No!'

This rule also applies if a speech is interrupted:

> 'No, I didn't,' Martin said. He paused to think for a moment. No, he had no recollection of sitting on a sandwich. 'No, I'm sure I didn't.'

We didn't start a new paragraph for *'No, I'm sure I didn't'* because it's still Martin talking. If each new sentence is on a new line, a reader might think it is Lucinda speaking and become totally confused about who is saying what.

Remember that the rule is: every change of speaker is signalled by a new paragraph. Don't start a new paragraph if no change of speaker has occurred.

All potential novelists please take note: even a speech that's several paragraphs long must begin with an opening quotation mark and end with a closing quotation mark. *Don't* put a closing quotation mark at the end of any paragraph within the speech. (The reader will think the next paragraph is a different person speaking.) You can, if you wish, begin each new paragraph with an opening quotation mark (to remind the reader that it's still part of the speech), but this is not essential. When the quotation is finished (at the end of the last paragraph), put the closing quotation mark.

Writing someone's thought

Humans have a little voice inside their heads, like a running commentary on the world that continues pretty much all day. Right now you're hearing a little voice saying, 'What? I don't have a little voice in my head! That's crazy.' See, you *do* have a little voice inside your head. It's your thoughts, the voice that punctuates your day! To create believable characters in fiction, you need to represent their thoughts as well as their words. So how do you punctuate a character's thoughts? Should you use quotation marks (as we did for the little voice we imagined running through your head)? Should you use italics?

Guess what? No single answer to that question is possible. But we're not going to leave you completely in the dark. We do have some advice that can help you, so listen up.

If your piece contains a lot of direct speech, using quotation marks for thoughts becomes very messy. Situations will occur where you'll need to use double quotation marks inside single quotation marks and, before too long, you're in punctuation overload. Similarly, using italics can make the text look very busy and alienate your reader. The best way to indicate thoughts is to leave them as plain text. Your reader will soon know what is direct speech and what is thought. The following conversation between Jeremy and his father demonstrates this for you:

> 'Your mother and I value your views. You know that, don't you son?'

> Sure. That's why my opinion about whether to go to Bali or Tasmania made such a difference that we spent four weeks looking at convict ruins and apple orchards. 'Yes, Dad.'

> 'Well, Jeremy, something big is about to happen.'

> 'Are we moving again?' That'd be right. Just when I'm actually enjoying being at school and I've found a way to handle that cranky neighbour who hates Metallica.

Creating Scare Quotes: Aerial Quotation Marks

To be honest, the name *scare quotes* is a bit of an oddity. They're not scary at all. They probably should be called 'ironic quotes' or 'so-called quotes'. When people are talking, they use their fingers to make little aerial quotation marks (scare quotes) around words as they come out of their mouths. In writing, scare quotes indicate that you wish to distance yourself from a word you're quoting, or that you're suspicious about its use:

> Damian phoned in sick. He's got the 'flu' again. (Everyone knows he's got a hangover.)

> This 'antique' table has woodworm holes that appear to have been made with a drill. (It isn't an antique at all.)

They may also be used with slang words or nicknames to show that the writer knows that it's not formal language or that a speaker isn't comfortable using the word:

> 'Is that what you'd call "cool"?' asked Clarence.

> 'Not unless I wanted to sound like you,' said Rob. 'It's "deadly".'

But scare quotes are often used when they have no meaning at all, and then they're irritating — or misleading. Consider this message on a shop window:

> We sell 'stamps'. (Are the people who wrote this sign selling postage stamps or is it a secret code for something else that they're pretending are stamps?)

A useful test is to take the scare quotes away and see whether you're still saying what you mean. If the sentence says the same thing without the scare quotes, leave the scare quotes out.

Chapter 10

Writing with Style

*L*earning the nitty-gritty of grammar initiates you into the universal clan of language lovers. Welcome. It also helps you to correct your errors or, better yet, to avoid making errors at all. That's wonderful. In this chapter, however, we stride bravely up to the junction of good grammar and good writing style and examine how the two are inextricably connected.

Building Better Sentences

You need to organise your language so that others receive your message exactly as you intend it. The way you combine and connect ideas into chunks of meaning called sentences is an important part of clear communication. Without even knowing it, you use the skills of *coordination* and *subordination* whenever you use English, so try to put these skills in the front of your mind. That way you can use them on purpose.

Pairing equal ideas: Coordination

Good coordination training enables footballers to use both their right and left feet to kick with force and accuracy. *Coordinating ideas* in writing ensures that ideas of equal value are organised in logically connected main clauses and sentences. The *coordinating conjunctions* (*and, but, so, nor, yet, neither ... nor*) connect words and ideas of equal importance. In Chapter 6 we look at how we can also use semicolons, colons and conjuncts (including *therefore, thus, nevertheless*) to connect equal ideas. This process of connecting equal ideas is called *coordination*.

The following shows what happens with all three methods of coordination:

> NO COORDINATION: Suddenly the rain stopped. The footpath sprang back to life with bustling bodies. I closed my umbrella. I began threading my way back to the office.

> COORDINATION WITH COORDINATING CONJUNCTIONS: Suddenly the rain stopped *and* the footpath sprang back to life with bustling bodies, *so* I closed my umbrella *and* began threading my way back to the office. (Notice that the subject *I* has been omitted from the last idea because both parts of the sentence have exactly the same subject so you don't need to repeat it.)

> COORDINATION WITH SEMICOLONS: Suddenly the rain stopped; the footpath sprang back to life with bustling bodies. I closed my umbrella; I began threading my way back to the office.

> COORDINATION WITH CONJUNCTS: Suddenly the rain stopped; consequently, the footpath sprang back to life with bustling bodies. I closed my umbrella; thereafter, I began threading my way back to the office.

Note: The last two paragraphs would be unlikely to make it into print if they weren't examples in a grammar book. They're a little clunky, but the point is that each method of coordination creates a different style of paragraph and has a different effect.

Read them aloud and you can hear that using only coordinating conjunctions leads to a long, flat sentence. Using only semicolons jolts the reader along with its jumpiness, but hinges ideas closely. Using only conjuncts makes the paragraph sound so formal that it could have been written in a police statement. What works best with coordination is to mix and match the three methods to create the style you want. Like this:

> VERSION 1: Suddenly the rain stopped; the footpath sprang back to life with bustling bodies. I closed my umbrella *and* began threading my way back to the office.

VERSION 2: Suddenly the rain stopped; consequently, the footpath sprang back to life with bustling bodies. I closed my umbrella *and then* I began threading my way back to the office.

VERSION 3: Suddenly the rain stopped *so* the footpath sprang back to life with bustling bodies. I closed my umbrella; I began threading my way back to the office.

These are just three possibilities. You can coordinate the ideas in many ways to create the exact meaning and impact you want.

Think about whether your piece is formal or informal. You're more likely to use conjuncts like *furthermore, moreover* or *nevertheless* in business writing than in a piece of fiction (unless you're creating a certain type of character and want to use words like this in the character's dialogue). And vary the connectors you choose. Don't restrict yourself to *and* if you mean *as well as, also, besides, too, on top of, along with* or *what's more.*

Coordinating unrelated or unequal ideas is like trying to make a sandwich with two differently sized pieces of bread. They don't fit together. Mismatches in sentences cause confusion because the ideas don't belong together. Also remember that stringing too many main clauses into just one sentence can bamboozle your reader because the way the ideas relate to each other becomes unclear. Finally, using only coordination can make your piece sound rather lacklustre. You're likely to engage your reader more effectively if you throw in some *subordination* — which is what we look at in the next section.

Demoting lesser ideas: Subordination

Not all ideas are equal. Some ideas outrank others and require *subordination*, which is the technique used to arrange the parts of a sentence that have different weight and importance. And here's something that won't shock you. Using *subordinating conjunctions* such as *because, since, as, unless, although* and *if* creates subordination of ideas.

As a general rule of subordination, the main idea goes in the *independent* or *main clause* of a sentence while the less significant information is relegated to the *dependent* or *subordinate clause.* Yes, using *subordinate clauses* achieves *subordination* in sentences. Who would have guessed?

(Check out Chapter 3 for the truth about clauses.) Here's an example of subordination at work. The main clauses are in italics:

> Although she felt guilty, *Lucinda rejected Rashid's invitation to dinner.*
>
> *Lucinda felt guilty* when she rejected Rashid's invitation to dinner.

The first example emphasises Lucinda's rejection of the invitation, while the second sentence stresses her guilt.

Subordination also involves using clauses beginning with pronouns such as *who, whom, whose, which, whatever, whichever* and *that* (called *relative clauses*). They carry information of lower rank than the idea expressed in a main clause. Sometimes, you can show that an idea isn't vitally important by shortening it from a clause to a phrase or even a single word. Here's how subordination works:

> NO SUBORDINATION: I arrived back at the office. Rashid was waiting outside the lift. His face was red. He looked distressed. I was worried. Rashid is usually so calm.
>
> SUBORDINATION WITH SUBORDINATING CONJUNCTIONS: I arrived back at the office *where* Rashid was waiting outside the lift. His face was red, *as if* he was distressed. I was worried *because* Rashid is usually so calm.
>
> SUBORDINATION WITH RELATIVE CLAUSES: I arrived back at the office. Rashid, *whose face was red*, was waiting outside the lift. He was distressed, *which worried me*. Rashid is usually so calm. (Notice that the relative clauses are inside commas because they contain non-essential information that can be removed from the sentence.)
>
> SUBORDINATION BY SHORTENING INFORMATION FROM CLAUSES: I arrived back at the office. Rashid, *usually so calm*, was waiting outside the lift, *red-faced and distressed*. I was worried. (The new descriptions are inside commas because they contain additional, non-essential information.)

The choices that you make about what information to put into the main clause and what to subordinate create different shades of meaning and emphasis. The order in which you put the information adds to this. Here are varied versions of the sample paragraph, each with a slightly different emphasis:

> VERSION 1: *When* I arrived back at the office, Rashid, *who is usually calm*, was waiting outside the lift, *red-faced and distressed*. I was worried.

> VERSION 2: I arrived back at the office *where* Rashid, *red-faced*, was waiting outside the lift. He was distressed, *which worried me because* he is usually so calm.

Be careful not to subordinate too many ideas in one sentence or your reader may lose track of the meaning. The following sentence, while grammatically correct, is confusing because it's too long:

> I was worried *when* I arrived back at the office *because* Rashid, *who is usually calm*, was waiting outside the lift, *red-faced and distressed*.

The main clause in this sentence is *I was worried* and all of the other information has been subordinated. Is that really the main idea of the sentence? And if it is, is your reader likely to see that it's the main point? Probably not, because it has been buried under an avalanche of extra information.

Creating logic with coordination and subordination

Good writing conveys precisely what you intend, no guessing or 'you know what I mean'-ing required. Using both coordination and subordination to connect sentence parts helps you to communicate clearly. By emphasising key ideas, subordinating less important information and balancing equal statements, you show your reader the exact relationships between the points you are making.

Here's an example of what happens when we mix the methods of connecting the ideas from the example paragraphs used in the two preceding sections on coordination and subordination. Remember, this is just one of many possible ways to connect the information. The subordinated ideas are in italics:

> Suddenly the rain stopped. The footpath sprang back to life with bustling bodies. *Closing my umbrella*, I began threading my way back to the office.

> *When I arrived back at the office*, Rashid, *red-faced and distressed* was waiting outside the lift. I was worried: Rashid is usually so calm.

Read the passage again and skip the bits in italics. See how only the extra bits of description are subordinated and the information the writer wants to emphasise are in the main clauses? The choice of punctuation also helps to isolate and connect the ideas. You've reached it: the intersection of grammar and style. Stride forth with confidence!

Having sentences of different lengths adds to the rhythm of what you write, which creates interest for your reader. Long sentences, with a mixture of subordinated ideas and coordinated elements (like this sentence) can slow down the pace of a piece of writing so that descriptions mimic the way our eyes or a movie camera move across a scene. Single idea sentences make a strong statement.

Alternate between long and short sentences. If you find you have written a string of long sentences, you can create more variety by cutting out wordy and repetitive phrases. You can also break some into shorter sentences. Be aware, however, that too many short sentences in a row can make your writing sound jerky and disconnected.

Use long sentences where you need to convey a lot of information or you want to describe something in detail. Use short sentences to make important points.

Varying sentence patterns

Sentences have patterns. The most common type of sentence begins with the 'doer' of the action (the subject) followed by the action (the verb) and then a little more information or detail to complete the thought (the complement). For more detailed information, Chapter 2 addresses subjects while Chapter 3 covers complements. Now, look back at the first sentence of this paragraph:

> Sentences (the subject/'doer') have (the verb/action) patterns (complement/information needed to complete the sentence).

Pieces created in only that pattern become dull. They sound monotonous. They lack colour or interest. The reader may even fall asleep. (Are you still awake? That was four sentences in a row that followed the basic pattern. Dull, huh?)

To create interest, take a sentence and shake it up a little; change the pattern; see what happens when the subject–verb pair is moved to the middle or even the end of the sentence.

> *Johnno ate* far too much at the pie night last night. (basic pattern)
>
> Last night at the pie night, *Johnno ate* far too much.
>
> Far too much was what *Johnno ate* at the pie night last night.
>
> Last night, *Johnno ate* far too much at the pie night.
>
> At the pie night last night, far too much was what *Johnno ate*.

They all sound a little different, don't they? Each sentence emphasises a different point by stressing different words. Making sure your sentences are in varying patterns helps you to stress the information you want people to notice. It also helps to keep your audience awake!

Finding the Right Voice: Active and Passive

Verbs can have two voices — and we're not talking about piercing, or whiny, or nasal or baritone, or husky type voices. With verbs, *voice* means the way the verb behaves with respect to its subject. Verbs are in either *active* or *passive voice*. Take a look at these two examples:

> 'The window *was broken* yesterday,' reported Richard, carefully tucking his cricket bat under the couch.

> 'I *broke* the window yesterday,' reported Richard, hoping that his parents wouldn't be too angry.

How do the two sentences differ? Well, in one case Richard is hoping he won't be blamed and in the other he's confessing. Grammatically, Richard's statement in the first version focuses on the receiver of the verb's action, the *window*, which received the action of the verb *was broken*. The verb is *passive* (in *passive voice*) because the subject of the sentence isn't the person or thing doing the action. Instead, the subject is the person or thing receiving the action of the verb. In the second version the verb is in the *active voice* because the subject (*I*) performed the action (*broke*). When the subject is acting or being, the verb is *active*.

To find the subject of a sentence, locate the verb and ask *who* or *what . . .?* (insert the verb). For more information on subjects and verbs refer to Chapter 2.

Here are some active and passive verbs:

> Lucinda *is convinced* by Damian to get a tattoo. (passive — clueless Lucinda is receiving the convincing)

> Rashid *talks* Lucinda out of it. (active — conservative Rashid is doing the talking)

> Damian *is tattooed* by Bill. (passive — badboy Damian is receiving the tattooing)

Some people loathe the passive voice. They insist that the active voice is direct, honest and more powerful, and that the passive is evasive and takes more words. In fact, sometimes the passive is not just acceptable: it's preferable. Everyone accepts that if you don't know the facts, the passive comes in handy:

> Little progress *has been made* in the investigation of the murder of Ms Stakes, the local teacher who *was battered* to death with her own garden gnome a year ago today. (This example, using passive voice, is 32 words. You'll notice that in passive voice, the verbs have auxiliaries. Parts of the verb *to be* are the auxiliary verbs in the passive voice — *has been, was.*)

The passive version doesn't say who has made little progress, but you can guess the subject is probably police. It has no specific information about the murderer because he (or she) hasn't been identified yet; the sentence contains all the information available.

Anti-passive-voice activists claim that using passive misleads people because it leaves out the performer of the verb (in this case, the police and the murderer). But this example isn't misleading at all. By not mentioning the police, the passive version emphasises the lack of progress, which is the problem. And, by not mentioning the murderer, it emphasises the crime, which is the newsworthy event. Opponents of passive voice also whine that it's more wordy than the forthright active voice. Well, here's the active-voice version:

> Police *have made* little progress in their investigation of the murder of Ms Stakes. An unknown assailant *battered* the local teacher to death with her own garden gnome a year ago today. (This active version has 32 words — okay, 30 if you say *someone* instead of *an unknown assailant.*)

Both versions are the same length, and the active voice version has neither the focus nor the impact of the passive version. Sometimes, choosing passive voice allows you to focus on what's most important.

But the strongest argument of the anti-passive-voice brigade is that the passive is evasive — it avoids giving information. Look at these sentences:

> It *has been recommended* that the servicing of the heating system be postponed until next year. (Passive: 16 words)

> Ron *recommended* that the servicing of the heating system be postponed until next year. (Active: 14 words)

In the first (passive) sentence, no-one is taking responsibility. If the central heating breaks down, nobody knows who to blame. In the second (active) sentence, the building's residents know exactly who to blame if they're freezing. It's all Ron's fault. Sometimes it's handy to be able to hide behind a passive sentence. Ask Ron!

Here are examples of when to choose the passive voice:

- ✔ if it's not clear who performed the action:

    The glass eye was found on the beach.

- ✔ if it's not necessary to know who or what performed the action:

    Sugar was added to the mixture.

- ✔ to emphasise the someone or something that suffered the action:

    The politician was forced to eat his own words.

- ✔ to create a sense of distance and avoid taking blame for the action:

    Your request for a refund has been denied.

If you're not trying to do any of the preceding, follow the advice of the anti-passive lobby and choose active voice. Active voice takes your reader in a straight line from one point to the other. Passive voice is less direct.

So what should you do if your grammar checker alerts you to the presence of passive voice and advises that you consider revising the sentence? Well, the obvious first port of call is to check your sentence against the preceding list of instances when passive voice is preferable. Then, if your sentence doesn't fit into any of those categories, here's an illustration of how to convert it to active voice:

The interview was conducted by Rupert himself.

Step one in the revision is to locate the verb group and remove the helping or auxiliary verb/s (we put a line through the word(s) to remove):

~~was~~ conducted

Step two is to locate the performer of the verb's action (the performer will be a noun or noun equivalent — but remember that sometimes in passive voice the performer of the verb's action isn't even mentioned, so you may have to add a subject). Then move the subject to the front of the main verb to create a subject–verb pair. You probably have to drop the preposition *by* completely:

> ~~by~~ *Rupert himself* ~~was~~ conducted

Step three is simply to add the rest of the sentence:

> Rupert himself conducted the interview.

You have now converted the sentence to active voice, with the subject performing the verb's action.

You want to avoid shifting from active to passive voice in the same sentence. Consider the following:

> My disgusting cat *stalks* drop-tail skinks and then their tails *are eaten* by her. (active + passive = wrong)

> Drop-tail skinks *are stalked* by my disgusting cat and then their tails *are eaten* by her. (passive + passive = correct but not a very good sentence — or a very pleasant habit for a cat to have, just quietly — because this sentence does not need to be passive)

> My disgusting cat *stalks* drop-tail skinks and then *eats* their tails. (active + active = correct and a better sentence)

Creating Writing That Flows: Cohesion

Have you ever been frustrated because even though you've included all the required information in your document and you're satisfied with the content, your piece still seems awkward and a bit disjointed — more like a bus trip than a ride in a luxury vehicle? Fear not; help is at hand. With understanding of how to create better connectedness, your writing can flow with the smooth ease of an Aston Martin.

For a wordsmith, *cohesion* refers to the way whole sentences and paragraphs are linked to each other. In a cohesive piece of writing, the sentences and paragraphs build on each other and grow in a logical way. Ideas flow and the reader can follow your message effortlessly. In the following sections, we cover sequencing and linking ideas.

Putting ideas in order: Sequencing

How hard can it be to get your ideas in the right order? Well, sometimes that's exactly what stumps writers. The best way to sequence and link information is from old or known information to new. Then, the new information at the end of one sentence becomes the old information for the sentence that follows, like this:

> William Dampier was very curious about what the world beyond England was like. *He* was *also curious* about plants, animals and the people he met on his travels. Observations about *these things* filled his journals.

The second sentence builds on the information in the first sentence by substituting *he* for William Dampier, using the connecting word *also* to connect ideas, and repeating the word *curious*. Then, the words *these things* link the third sentence to the second sentence by summarising the words *plants, animals and the people he met*. That's *cohesion* at a sentence level.

Cohesion of paragraphs creates the structure for a piece of writing. The best way to do this depends on what you're writing. Here are some logical ways to sequence ideas:

- past to present to future
- general to specific
- simple to complicated
- best to worst
- ideal to actual
- problem to solution
- question to answer
- idea to example
- data or findings to conclusions.

Think about what you're writing and why, and then choose a suitable technique to put your ideas in order. If you're writing a technical report, you may move from findings to conclusions, whereas for a short story, you could opt for a chronological (then until now) approach.

Connecting ideas with transition words

Like a story that's impossible to put down, or an argument that's so logical it changes what you've always thought, good writers link the ideas in their sentences and connect their sentences into paragraphs that lead to a logical conclusion. One of the ways they do this is with *signpost words*, sometimes also called *transition words*, such as *therefore*, *apparently*, *similarly*, *finally*. They signal the relationships between ideas to help readers navigate the document. Here's an example with the transition words in italics:

> Cat-lovers have many reasons for preferring cats to dogs. *Firstly*, feline friends are quieter than canine companions, *thus* far less annoying to neighbours. And *secondly*, cats are infinitely cleaner than dogs. *After all*, you don't have to carry poop bags around when you have a cat or bathe them to eliminate their dreadful smell.
>
> *By contrast*, dog defenders argue that cats don't prevent burglaries or protect vehicles. *Furthermore*, cats cause much discomfort to allergy sufferers. *In fact*, very few people find themselves wheezing and sneezing in the presence of dogs; *however*, the allergen in cat spit affects millions.

Notice how commas and/or semicolons accompany the signpost words. They are like extra links added to a chain of words (the sentence) and, if you remove them, the meaning is unchanged.

The following table of signpost words can help you create logical links in your writing.

Link Required	*Words to Choose*
Adding to or continuing	additionally, again, also, as well as, besides, coupled with, furthermore, in addition to this, in the same way, moreover, too
Comparing	by comparison, correspondingly, in the same way, likewise, moreover, similarly
Showing cause or consequence	accordingly, as a result, consequently, for this reason, hence, therefore, thus
Contrasting	alternatively, by contrast, conversely, despite that, even though, instead, nevertheless, on the contrary, on the other hand, otherwise, rather
Showing chronology	afterward, during, earlier, first of all, following that, formerly, later on, meanwhile, next, previously, secondly, simultaneously, subsequently, the next step, to begin with
Giving examples or explaining	exemplifying this, for example, for instance, including, indeed, in fact, in particular, namely, specifically, such as, that is, thus, to illustrate
Showing exceptions	apart from, aside from, barring, excluding, other than, with the exception of
Summarising or concluding	after all, all in all, finally, in any case, in conclusion, in short, on balance, on the whole, to sum up

Choose wisely from this list to connect your sentences into paragraphs and your paragraphs into longer pieces of writing. By doing so, you take your reader with you on the journey from start to finish.

Being Absolutely Clear: Plain English

Few things are more frustrating than trying to decode a document that's so chock-a-block with technical words and long sentences that you have to read it several times to get the message. You want your reader to thank you for communicating with them, not curse you. Writing that speaks directly to the reader, and is clear and concise is described as *plain English*, and it's a perfect example of the overlap of style and grammar.

Plain English sentences are always written in *active voice* (active and passive voice are discussed in the section 'Finding the Right Voice: Active and Passive' earlier in this chapter), are thoughtfully coordinated and subordinated (discussed in the section 'Building Better Sentences' earlier in this chapter), and carefully punctuated. Whole books have been written about it; organisations are dedicated to it. Here, we provide a quick look at the basics of plain English.

Avoiding word-wasting

Having to write formal documents such as job applications, workplace reports and essays for tertiary studies often brings on a bad case of verbal diarrhoea. It's a fair bet that one of the reasons for this is that people think wordy, ornate writing sounds formal in the way that legal documents do. In reality, using unnecessarily flowery language just sounds like pompous bafflegab. Plain English demands that you should never use more words than you need. Table 10-1 shows some examples of unnecessarily flowery language, and what they can be replaced with.

Table 10-1	Ways to Use Plain English
Unnecessary Language	*Replace With*
at the present moment	now
for the purpose of	for
in the event of	if
in the majority of circumstances	usually, generally, mostly
in respect of	about
make an application	apply
on account of the fact that	because
provide an explanation	explain
with the minimum of delay	immediately, quickly

And here are some flabby sentences with their plain language counterparts:

> WRONG: If there are any issues about which you require further information or particulars, we shall be glad to provide any additional details by telephone.
>
> RIGHT: Please call if you have any queries.
>
> WRONG: It is important for you to remember the limited capacity for attention of many members of the reading public and thus the relative importance of choosing words and sentence structures that fit together in a dynamic way to keep your audience's attention focused.
>
> RIGHT: Remember that readers bore easily, so choose dynamic words and sentence structures that engage your audience.

Sometimes the excess baggage in a document comes with *clichés* — expressions that are overused and dull. In fact, sometimes people who work together communicate in expressions that are almost meaningless. Plain English is direct and fresh:

> WRONG: I write to place before you my application for the position of trainee Jedi knight as advertised in *The Galactic Times.*
>
> RIGHT: As a huge fan of the Force, I dream of training as a Jedi knight.
>
> WRONG: For the project we currently have on the front burner, it will be necessary to massage the material thoroughly before putting it to bed.
>
> RIGHT: We will need to edit this project carefully.

Wordy documents waste people's time. Your reader won't get bogged down in a plain English success story because it communicates without being flowery or verbose.

Deciding when a sentence has too many words is like responding to the question, 'How long is a piece of string?' Answer: As long as it needs to be. The recommendation for plain Aussie English, however, is that if the average length of your sentences is more than 22 words, you're overdoing it. Pull back. A 15 to 20 word average is plenty.

Selecting the best words

You will have noticed that employing a functional interface benchmark (FIB) and leading-edge impactful energetics (LIE) can improve your base-level efficiency. You haven't? Well, of course not, because neither those gobbledygook word combinations nor the acronyms they form (FIB and LIE) exist. They do, however, demonstrate one of the enemies of plain English: trendy language and jargon. This is almost meaningless language often shared between people who work in the same field or share an interest. Plain English demands that everyone be able to understand your document, not just someone who thinks and speaks exactly as you do. Choose clear everyday words over complex specialised ones.

One of the most helpful, friendly features you have in your word processor (even more friendly than those cute little guys hidden in the Help facility) is the thesaurus that just drops out of the tool bar at the click of a mouse. Or, if you prefer, you can make friends with a thesaurus in good old-fashioned book form. A thesaurus gives you alternatives to the words you've written (or are about to write), plus a range of similar words, and even opposites. Finding the exact word to express your meaning is that easy.

However, don't just throw in any word from the list your thesaurus suggests. You don't want to perturb your audience with an anomalous and expeditious permutation in your mode of interchange. Choose words that fit comfortably with the rest of your plain English piece.

Staying positive

Remaining positive is another feature of plain language — not positive as in your frame of mind but positive as in your word choice. Positive words are easier to understand because they require only one thought process; you don't have to think about what a word means and then work out the opposite meaning. Table 10-2 shows negative constructions and how they can be made positive.

Table 10-2 Negative versus Positive Constructions

Negative	Positive
fail to notice	overlook
not dissimilar	similar
not the same	different
unfinished	ongoing, continuing
untrue	false

And here's an example sentence, showing negative and then positive word choice:

> WRONG: Just under half of the team didn't know the address of the oval.

> RIGHT: Over half of the team knew the address of the oval.

Finally, don't use a noun where a verb would fit. Verbs communicate more clearly and make your writing livelier. The nouns and corresponding verbs are in italics in the following examples:

> WRONG: We need *clarification* of exactly what *improvements* will be made upon the *implementation* of your plan. (Notice that this is also in passive voice.)

> RIGHT: Please *clarify* exactly what you *will improve* when you *implement* your plan. (This version is in active voice.)

Being concise doesn't mean being brief. It means choosing the best word, using the active voice, and creating documents that are understood at first reading. Master plain English and that job you dream of is much more likely to be yours. May the Force be with you!

Chapter 11

Creating More Accurate Documents

* *

In This Chapter

▶ Writing accurate bullet point lists

▶ Punctuating addresses and dates

▶ Considering abbreviations, acronyms and initialisms

▶ Structuring formal emails

▶ Creating professional visual presentations

▶ Presenting information in bibliographies

* *

*W*hile it's true that pretty much everyone now writes with a computer, it's also true that not everyone is confident about what they create when doing so. Don't panic. In this chapter, we're here to help unravel some of the mysteries of e-grammar and formal writing. Before long, you'll be sending only the clearest of emails through cyberspace and preparing documents that impress all who look upon them.

Summarising with Bullet Point Lists

When it comes to summarising information and setting it out clearly, bullet point lists rule. In this section, we show you current Australian style for punctuating these lists.

Most bullet point lists begin with part of a sentence, and then each point completes that sentence. In grammarspeak, the points are *sentence fragments*. So, each point must match up with the opening statement to form a correct sentence when the two parts are read together. Here's an example of this type of bullet point list that shows you how they're punctuated:

Please take note of the:

- colon at the end of the introductory words
- lower case (not capital) letter at the start of each point
- absence of punctuation at the end of the point up until now
- full stop at the end of the last point.

Always make sure that the points in your list are grammatically equal (*parallel construction* is the official way to describe it in grammar-guru circles — refer to Chapter 8 for more). The points should all start with the same part of speech, either a clear noun or a strong verb. And your lead-in statement, the bit before the points, should be direct and clear. Here's an example of a list with a weak lead-in statement and points that aren't parallel:

There are lots of different aspects to being a good writer:

- skill with grammar
- imagination
- take criticism.

This list fails because the lead-in contains a passive verb when it should have an active verb. (Refer to Chapter 10 for more on passive and active verbs.) And it's not parallel because the first two points begin with a noun, while the final point begins with a verb (take). Here's how the lists should look:

Starting with Nouns

Being a good writer requires:

- skill with grammar
- imagination
- willingness to take and act on criticism.

Starting with Verbs

Being a good writer requires you to:

- demonstrate skill with grammar
- display imagination
- accept and respond to criticism.

Read through your list and connect the opening statement to each point in turn. This helps you check that the grammar of your list is accurate because, with your expertly trained ear and extensive knowledge of correct sentence structure, you will immediately detect any problems.

Sometimes a bullet point list is not a sentence with several possible endings. Instead, it is a string of separate items. Punctuate a list of items the same way as the examples already included in this section:

Qualities of good presentations:

- carefully chosen words

- appropriate graphics

- excellent use of bullet points.

If the points you're making need to come in a particular order, use numbers instead of bullets. (See the section 'Ensuring Effective Emails' later in this chapter and you can see this style in action.) It's also useful to number your points if you know you need to refer back to them at a later stage. This means you can professionally remind your audience about the information in 'point two of the previous slide' rather than make the vague reference 'as I said before'.

Finally, if the points in your list are complete sentences, they keep their capital letters and full stops. Like this:

Rashid made two important discoveries:

- Lucinda cares more for herself than she does for anyone else.

- Falling in love can lead to embarrassing situations.

Creating clear bullet point lists improves the quality of your presentations. (See the section 'Focussing on Visual Presentations' later in this chapter for more.)

Handling Addresses and Dates

These days, when people write letters, they mean business. Knowing the way to present and punctuate addresses and dates is crucial to impressing the reader.

Adding addresses

When typing the address at the top of a letter and putting it on the envelope, it should look like this in both places:

Bestseller Publishers Ltd

223 Print Street

Booksville Readersland 1234

Each item has a line of its own if room is available. If it isn't, put a comma between any items you're combining, except the suburb or town, state and postcode on the last line.

If you put the address into a sentence, you have to separate each item of the address, except the postcode:

Bryce's publisher has an office at 223 Print Street, Booksville, Readersland 1234.

If the sentence continues, you should separate the last item in the address from the rest of the sentence with another comma:

Bryce's publisher has an office at 223 Print Street, Booksville, but the company is moving to Pagetown next month.

Dealing with the date

At least seven ways to write the date exist:

28 September 2097

28/9/97 (or 28/09/97)

September 28, 2097

Sept. 28th, 2097

28.09.97 (or 28.9.97)

You only need a comma where you put two numbers next to each other without any other sort of punctuation. Never put a comma between the date and the name of the month. You don't need a comma after the day of the week either (Wednesday 28 September).

The best choice for letter writing is the first example in the preceding list (28 September 2097). Because the sequence from day to month to year is logical, it doesn't need any punctuation, and it avoids any possible confusion from having numbers side by side.

If you're sending letters all over the world, remember that people put the information in a different order in other countries, which can lead to confusion. In the United States, for example, 6/10 means 10 June, not 6 October as it does in Australia and the United Kingdom. And in Japan 08.09.05 means 5 September 2008. So it's a good idea to write the month and year in full, in whatever order you put the day, month and year.

To insert a date into a sentence, you may need one more comma:

> On 28 September 2097, Gael ate three boxes of chocolates.

or

> Gael was especially quiet for an hour on 28 September 2097, when she ate three boxes of chocolates.

Filling in the Rules for Abbreviations

Formal writing implies thought and care, not haste. Abbreviations fit comfortably in informal documents like text messages and personal emails, but few of them are welcome in official documents. Later in this chapter, we look at how to use abbreviations in bibliographies — an acceptable home for abbreviations in formal communication. Another place they inhabit comfortably is tables or charts of data. Apart from that, treat them with suspicion and use them sparingly when you're being businesslike.

So, now that you know why you shouldn't abbreviate, here's how to do it correctly if you decide it's appropriate:

✔ put a full stop on the end of abbreviations formed by removing the end of the word — the Rev. Thomson, Fig. 8, vol. 2

✔ don't put a full stop on the end of an abbreviation formed by removing the middle of the word but leaving both ends (contractions) — Mrs Edwards (Mrs dates from a time when women were addressed as Mistress), Dr Jones, Jeremiah Jones Jnr, St Francis, High St, Station Rd

✔ don't put a full stop after abbreviations made from the first letters of a number of words in capitals — UK, USA, ABC

✔ use a full stop for a word abbreviated to one capital letter — R. (river)

✔ don't put full stops after the initials in someone's name — C J Dennis

✔ use Australian style for days: Mon. Tues. Wed. Thurs. Fri. Sat. Sun.

✔ use Australian style for months, which is only to abbreviate those months with more than four letters in their name, and then add a full stop: Jan. Feb. Mar. Apr. Aug. Sept. Oct. Nov. Dec.

✔ keep the abbreviations in a company name: John Wiley & Sons.

✔ 30 s, 1 min, 2 h are the abbreviations for 30 seconds, 1 minute, 2 hours — these are preferable to secs, mins and hrs in all contexts

✔ m, km, cm stand for metre, kilometre, centimeter.

Stretching out acronyms

Business writing and journalism are positively littered with *acronyms* — new words made from a string of the first letters of each word in a multi-word title (sometimes with a few other letters thrown in for good measure). To qualify as an acronym, the group of letters must have become so well known that people pronounce it as a word. Some common acronyms are:

AIDS: Acquired Immune Deficiency Syndrome

ASIO: Australian Security Intelligence Organisation

HECS: Higher Education Contribution Scheme

PIN: Personal Identification Number

RAM: Random Access Memory

Most acronyms consist of capital letters without full stops between them. Others, however, survive long enough that all but their initial capital letter shrinks to lower case, like Anzac and Qantas. Some lucky acronyms become so widespread that they are granted a new life and morph into regular words, even losing their initial capital letter. Two of these blessed acronyms are radar (Radio Detecting And Ranging) and scuba (Self-Contained Underwater Breathing Apparatus). The transformation from acronym to word is an ongoing process; for example, AIDS is becoming Aids. If you're not sure what to do with an acronym, check a current Australian dictionary.

Clearing up initialisms

Other common abbreviations made up from the first letter of a group of words are called initialisms. We don't pronounce them as words but as separate letters. Abbreviations such as CD (compact disc) and NPO (non-profit organisation) fit into this category.

You should always know your audience and use language that's appropriate for their level of understanding of the topic you're discussing. The same goes for abbreviations. To avoid any misunderstandings, especially in official documents, write the words in full the first time you use an acronym such as HECS (Higher Education Contribution Scheme), or an initialism such as GST (Goods and Services Tax) and then put the abbreviation after it in brackets (the opposite of what we have just done). This helps minimise the TCQ (total confusion quotient) of what you write.

Ensuring Effective Emails

Electronic communication was once thought of as informal and snail-mail was preferred for anything formal. Not any more. Email is routinely used for job applications, office memos, letters of complaint, resignations — all types of formal communication. Emails are even admissible as evidence in legal cases. So in the following section, we cover how to get email out of its boardshorts and into a business suit.

Establishing who, why and what

Something about the speed and immediacy of emails causes people to respond to them quickly — sometimes too quickly. You need to think about who it is you're writing to and exactly why you're writing to them. If you don't, your email could have an inappropriate tone or be too casual. Plus, messages written in haste are often unclear and can be misinterpreted by the receiver.

Then, after the who and why, consider what you want the recipient to do after reading the message. File it? Ignore it? Send it on? Take action? Attend an event? Here's how to get the job done with an email:

1. **Ensure your subject line is clear.**

   The first thing the recipient of your message will see, other than your name, is the subject line. Be sure that it clearly describes the reason for the message. It should represent your main purpose for writing. Treat it as a title or heading and use capital letters accordingly (refer to Chapter 7 for details about how to do this). Think about whether your heading is likely to make it easy for other people to file your message correctly or find again. Don't put 'Meeting' if what you mean is 'Planning Meeting Details'.

2. **Include a greeting with the person's name.**

   Including a greeting is polite. You can use *Hello Clare* or *Hi Tran* if you're writing to a colleague you know well. However, stick with the traditional way of opening if you're dealing with someone much higher up the pecking order than you — *Dear Ms Bossibootz*, or *Dear Christiana* if you usually call the person by their first name (no punctuation following and then drop down a line). (Use their real name, of course!)

3. **Jump right in with the key point.**

   The most important part of your message must come in the first paragraph.

4. **Don't waste words; it wastes the reader's time.**

   Write in short sentences and paragraphs but don't use the abbreviations you might put into a text message. Using active voice helps to make your message sound direct and concise. *We are meeting* is better than *There will be a meeting.*

5. **Outline what you expect from the recipient in your second paragraph.**

   What action do you expect from them? And by when? Or, if you're just giving information, add more detail to what you said in the first paragraph. Doing this in point form can help to keep your message clear and brief (refer to the section 'Summarising with Bullet Point Lists' earlier in this chapter).

   Choose positive language when outlining what you expect people to do. People are likely to take action if you say: *Please respond by Thursday so that your ideas can be included on the agenda.* They're not going to be persuaded by the negative version: *If you fail to respond by Thursday, your ideas will not be included on the agenda.*

6. **List any attachments to the message.**

   This gives the reader something to check, and helps to remind you to actually attach the attachments!

7. **Sign off appropriately.**

   It's not polite to just end with your signature block. The traditional way to end formal communications is with *Yours sincerely* if you know the person's name but not much more about them, *Kind regards* or *Regards* if you know them on a first name basis, and *Yours faithfully* if you don't know them at all.

8. **Before you hit send, double-check everything.**

   Check the subject line, proofread and tidy up the message, and confirm the list of recipients to make sure your email only goes to the people who need to receive it.

Averting potential disaster

Hands up if you've ever sent an email zinging off through cyberspace at exactly the same moment that a little voice in your head said, 'OMG ... did I just ...'. You can put your hand down again now. Wouldn't want you to drop this fabulously useful book. Well, fear no more. Follow these helpful hints and you'll never have to worry about email disaster again:

- Never try to be funny. It's bound to end in tears. Remember that the reader can't see the look on your face, so your humour may lead to miscommunication. Use straightforward, plain English.

- Apply the 'Granny Rule'. If you wouldn't want your gran to read it, don't write it. Keep yourself nice.

- Add the subject line after you've written the message. Your description of the purpose of the email is going to be far more accurate if you've completed writing the content. You'll summarise what you actually wrote, not describe what you meant to write.

- Enter the address of the recipient/s last, after you've checked and proofread the message. You're far less likely to send something that contains errors or has gaps in the information if you review the content before adding the addresses.

- Send really important messages to yourself first. That way, you can see if the email arrives in the correct format and with all the attachments in place.

When writing an official email, treat it as if you were going to print out the communication to post in the way your ancestors used to send birthday cards — in an envelope with a stamp.

Focussing on Visual Presentations

Visual presentations, even in an educational or work situation, provide the means for you to mix words and graphics to communicate with your audience. Here you can check out how to put together presentation slides that will spin some magic.

Keep it simple. When preparing your presentation, it's important to remember that the slides are not your presentation — they are prompts for you, the presenter, to use. They're supposed to focus the attention of the audience while you talk, not provide all the important detail. That's your job.

Here are some basics to help you prepare presentation slides that are clear and effective:

✔ Restrict the number of words you use. Experts differ about how much text is too much, but the *six times six rule* is a good guideline. Include no more than six words per line and six lines per slide. Slides with too much text are boring, and besides, the more words you use, the smaller they are on the screen. And the smaller they are, the less useful they are to your audience.

✔ Have only one idea per slide.

✔ Summarise information into point form or even single words. (The section 'Summarising with Bullet Point Lists' earlier in this chapter explains the correct way to use bullet points.)

✔ Use graphics. Many people read pictures more quickly and clearly than words. So, presenting information as a chart or diagram is a good way of communicating with them. Adding an image can also help people remember the point you're making. Cute animal pics or funny cartoons that distract from the information don't work; choose something that reinforces your message. A strong chain could illustrate a message about teamwork; a pair of scissors can reinforce information about the need for editing.

✔ Restrict yourself to no more than three fonts: one for the heading, one for body text and another for tables is more than enough. Switching fonts looks busy and amateurish. Using fonts consistently adds authority to your presentation.

✔ Choose a colour scheme with contrast so your words are easy to read, and use no more than two or three colours. Multi-coloured slides are distracting. You want the audience to be thinking about what you're presenting, not wondering what colour combination is coming next. Something like white letters on a dark blue background works well.

✔ Avoid being too tricky with effects such as animation and transitions between slides. Again, it's distracting if your words and images are flying and cartwheeling on and off the screen in random patterns. It also looks childish and unprofessional. Choose a couple of effects and use them consistently. Having points appear one after the other, for example, is a useful addition to your presentation.

Remember that your slides don't need to say everything. They need only to suggest everything, and remind you what to say. You're the presenter. The slides are there to support you, not replace you.

Presenting Perfect Bibliographies

Only so many ideas exist in the world and happily (or perhaps not-so-happily, depending on your point of view) other people have already written about most of them. So, when your turn to produce a written piece rolls around, chances are you're going to start with what's already out there. Whenever you do this, you need to acknowledge those other thinkers by creating a list (or bibliography) of the things you read or watched or listened to before you began writing.

Bibliographies take many different forms, and institutions and organisations have their own preferences; for the fine print, you should always check with your style guide. In the following section, we have a peek at the basics of two main styles: the author–date and the documentary–note systems.

You need to acknowledge all kinds of information sources. Books, magazines and journals, encyclopaedias, podcasts, DVDs, websites, newspaper articles, interviews, television programs — list all of them in your bibliography.

Sometimes finding the details you need to record can be tricky, but that's no excuse. Look harder! Books have imprint pages just in from the front cover; websites have addresses, home pages and often 'about us' pages, many with details at the very bottom; interviews take place somewhere at some specific time and are viewed or heard on a particular media outlet; ebooks are located on a specific database or website; and many digitised articles have a DOI (digital object identifier), which is a more permanent internet address than a URL. Collect information as if performing a treasure hunt.

Understanding author–date system versus documentary–note system

For both the author–date system (the Harvard style fits into this system) and the documentary–note system (the Oxford system belongs in this category), you must include the same information. The differences lie in the order in which you put that information and the punctuation that you use. With bibliographies, every little thing matters.

Essentially, what you must record is author, title, volume number, publisher, date and place of publication, the numbers of the pages you read, or a website URL address or DOI.

Table 11-1 provides examples of how to set out the information, depending on the system you're using. So, get out your magnifying glass and pay close attention to each and every comma, space, full stop, use of italics and capital letter. Your sources may not have all of the details we've included in the model entries, but your bibliography should contain as many as possible.

By the way, we've used minimal capitalisation for the author–date system and maximal capitalisation for the documentary–note system. You can choose whichever you prefer, or check with your style guide.

Defining a reference list

Don't confuse a bibliography with a reference list. Both are records of information sources and both come at the end of your document. The essential difference between the two is that while a bibliography lists everything you checked out during your research, whether or not you mention it, a reference list names only the sources to which you directly refer in your piece.

You present an author–date reference list exactly as you would a bibliography in this system (as shown in Table 11-1). A reference list in documentary–note style differs from a bibliography. You don't list sources in alphabetical order according to the author's surname. Instead, you number them, and put them in the order in which you refer to them within your document. So, within a reference list in this system, the first author's initials come before the surname and are separated from the surname by a space. This should help:

WM Anderson & G Woods, (reference list entry)

Anderson, WM & G Woods, (bibliography entry)

Table 11-1	Setting Out Information Using the Author–Date and Documentary–Note Systems	
	Author–Date System	*Documentary–Note System*
Book 1 author	Gumly, M 2013, *Exceptional eucalypts*, 2nd edn, Acacia & Sons Publishers, Frenchs Forest, pp. 279–312.	Gumly, M, *Exceptional Eucalypts*, 2nd edn, Acacia & Sons Publishers, Frenchs Forest, 2013, pp. 279–312.
Book 2 authors	Spiker, AB & Beaky, IC 2012, *Echidna breeding*, 4th edn, Prickly Publishers, Yackandandah.	Spiker, AB & IC Beaky, *Echidna Breeding*, 4th edn, Prickly Publishers, Yackandandah, 2012.
Article in an edited book	Winger, U 2011, 'Kindred kestrels' in EA Falconer (ed), *Winged hunters*, Sky Books, Perth, pp. 19–31.	Winger, U, 'Kindred Kestrels' in EA Falconer (ed.), *Winged Hunters*, Sky Books, Perth, 2011, pp. 19–31.
Print article	Flipperforth, WH 2013, 'Dolphins at a glance', *Deepsea Review*, vol. 41, no. 1, pp. 6–21.	Flipperforth, WH, 'Dolphins at a Glance', *Deepsea Review*, vol. 41, no. 1, 2013, pp. 6–21.
Electronic copy of article on database	Shelby, H 2010, 'Terrapin talk', *Oceans Weekly*, 10 March, p.16, viewed 19 May 2014, Database C online.	Shelby, H, 'Terrapin Talk', *Oceans Weekly*, 10 March 2010, p.16, retrieved 19 May 2014, Database C.
Electronic copy of article with DOI	Hopper, C 2006, 'Wandering wallabies: a geographic study', *Journal of Marsupials*, vol 2, pp. 61–79, DOI:10.2377/6988602105018757	Hopper, C, 'Wandering Wallabies: A Geographic Study', *Journal of Marsupials*, vol. 2, 2006, pp. 61–79, DOI:10.2377/6988602105018757
e-book	Common, HN 2009, *Encounters with wombats*, Bush Press, viewed 9 May 2014, Bookz 24x7, <http://www.bookz24x7.org/etext9/2h.htm>.	Common, HN, *Encounters with Wombats*, Bush Press, 2009, retrieved 9 May 2014, Bookz 24x7, <http://www.bookz24x7.org/etext9/2h.htm>

	Author–Date System	*Documentary–Note System*
Web document with author	Barker, K 2011, Dingo details, Barker Network, viewed 11 May 2014, <http://www.barkernet.org/dindets.html>	Barker, K, Dingo Details, Barker Network, 2011, retrieved 11 May 2014, <http://www.barkernet.org/dindets.html>
Web document without author	*Roo racing made easy* 2014, Crazy Corporation, viewed 11 May 2014, <http://www.crazcorp.org/racing/roo-report.html>	*Roo Racing Made Easy*, Crazy Corporation, viewed 11 May 2014, <http://www.crazcorp.org/racing/roo-report.html>
DVD	*Effective flea control* 2010 [DVD], Critter Productions Australasia, Adelaide.	*Effective Flea Control*, DVD, Critter Productions Australasia, Adelaide, 2010.

Chapter 12

Ten Solutions to the Most Common Grammar Errors

*N*obody's perfect. We all make mistakes and, quite honestly, the English language is so tricky that tripping up is easy. So, in this chapter, we look at ten common grammar hiccups — the sort that inspire your grammar checker to decorate your documents with wiggly green lines and helpfully suggest that you consider revising your words. Here, we take the next step and show you how to make those revisions.

Adding Apostrophes (Or Not)

If apostrophes were people, they'd all need regular counselling. They're the most misunderstood and abused of all punctuation marks. You can help rebuild their self-esteem by remembering that *it's* means *it is* or *it has* in the same way that *she's* means *she is* or *she has*, and *he's* means *he is* or *he has*. Under no circumstances and in no instance does *it's* ever mean belonging to it. *Its* without the apostrophe means belonging to it. Always. In every case. No exception with that one. You'd never put an apostrophe in *his*, *hers* or *ours* (meaning belonging to him, her or us), so don't put one in *its* — unless you mean *it is* or *it has*.

The second most common apostrophe catastrophe involves confusion about where to put the little wiggle when the word you want to turn into a possessive ends in the letter *s*. (A *possessive* is, of course, a word that shows ownership.) The solution is simple. Apply the always rules and you can't be wrong. Always add apostrophe + *s* when the word you want to turn into a possessive is singular (one thing). Yes, that's right, always — even if the word ends in *s*, as in *Jess's frown* or *cactus's spike*. It may look odd, but it isn't wrong. And always add the apostrophe after the *s* if the word is plural (more than one thing). Again, *the Joneses' contribution* might look weird, but if the contribution was made by all of the Joneses, the apostrophe is in the right place. (Chapter 6 deals with apostrophes.)

Reaching Agreement

The rule is simple. All verbs must match up with their subjects (the *who* or *what* performing the verb); all pronouns must match up with their antecedents (the word the pronoun stands in for). That's what this kind of agreement is; everybody in the Land of Sentence pairs up agreeably with the appropriate partner. Nobody is left standing alone in a corner and, most certainly, nobody tries to match up with somebody else's partner.

Thus, if the subject is singular (just one), so are the verb and the pronoun: *The author lost her mind.* And if the subject is plural (more than one), so are the verb and the pronoun: *Authors lose their minds.*

When the whole thing gets murky is when the subject looks singular but means something plural, or vice versa. We say *The staff wants improved conditions* (singular) because even though lots of staff members are in the company, they're acting as one united body. We say *The staff want to bring their partners to the function* (plural) because the staff is acting as individuals: presumably they don't all share one partner. To help decide in such cases, try putting the words *The whole* (staff, team, committee or whatever) in front of the verb. If your sentence makes sense that way, you need a singular verb. (Chapters 2 and 4 cover agreement.)

Staying in the Right Tense

Okay, listen up. Illegally switching tenses within a piece of writing is a common problem that can prove fatal. You must avoid unauthorised movement between past, present and future tense. To be clear about that: verbs have three main tenses. In the *past tense* something happened. In the *present tense*, something happens. In the *future tense*, something will happen. Sometimes, jumping from one tense to the other is necessary to put your communication in the correct time frame but, mostly, whatever you're writing should stay with just one tense.

Two tricks could help you with this. You can keep looking back at the verbs you've chosen earlier in the document to remind you what tense you should be using. Alternatively, picture what you're writing about as events marked on a time line with the central point being 'now — present tense'. That should help you decide which tense is needed. (Chapter 2 has more information about verbs than you could poke a stick at, and Chapter 8 delves further into shifting tenses.)

Splicing Sentences with a Comma

When you splice two pieces of rope together, you twist the frayed ends into one and hope the join will hold. When you splice two complete, independent ideas together with a comma, you create a join that cannot hold. We call this error a *comma splice*.

The comma is a weakling that never learned how to tie a double fisherman's knot. If you want to join two complete ideas, use a conjunction (joining word) or a punctuation mark with holding power: a semicolon. Complete ideas joined with a semicolon look like this: *Nicole loves to sing; Joel hates to listen.* Joined with a conjunction, they would be something like *Nicole loves to sing but Joel hates to listen.* (Chapter 6 handles the correct use of commas and semicolons, while conjunctions crop up in Chapter 10.)

Running Sentences On

The comma splice (refer to preceding section) has a sibling: the *run-on sentence*. This problem child comes to visit when you make no attempt to create a join or link between complete ideas, but instead simply dump them, nose-to-tail, in one sentence. You can eliminate this monster in exactly the same ways that you banish a comma splice, with a conjunction or a semicolon. Have a look at the example in the preceding section for information about how to use semicolons or conjunctions to be rid of this pest. The solution is the same. (Chapter 6 shows you the correct way to join ideas with punctuation marks: the colon and its relative the semicolon hold the key.)

Fragmenting Sentences

A meaningful group of words that begins with a capital letter and ends with a full stop is not necessarily a sentence. To qualify as a fully certified sentence, the group of words must contain a matching subject–verb pair. Without that pair, what you have is not a sentence but a sentence fragment.

Over the bridge, past the station and towards her favourite bookshop is a sentence fragment. Who did what in that sentence? We don't know. So, to revise it into a legitimate sentence, we must add a matching subject–verb pair. *Charlotte saunters over the bridge, past the station and towards her favourite bookshop.* Now we have a sentence. (Chapter 3 gets down to the nitty-gritty of complete sentences and fragments.)

Misplacing Modifiers

Putting a modifier in the wrong place is like hanging a magnificent piece of art over a window or opposite a crooked mirror. The artwork loses its impact in the confusion of too much glare or a distorted reflection. Misplaced modifiers are descriptions that have been put in the wrong place, like this: *Lucinda was walking the dog in her new stilettos.* While it's altogether possible that Lucinda has a female dog, and that Lucinda would humiliate the poor thing by making it wear shoes, it's highly unlikely that the dog could manage stilettos. So, to revise a sentence that contains a misplaced modifier, move the description closer to the word/s it's modifying, like this: *Lucinda, in her new stilettos, was walking the dog.* (Chapter 5 shows you how to create accurate descriptions with the correct placement of modifiers.)

Knowing When to Use Subject and Object Pronouns

The subject pronouns are *I, you, he, she, it, we* and *they.* The object pronouns are *me, you, him, her, it, us* and *them.* This may sound obvious, but you should choose a subject pronoun when a pronoun is the subject of the verb in your sentence (remember that you find the subject by asking the question '*Who* or *what* is performing or being the verb?'). Choose an object pronoun for everything else. (If this tip isn't obvious enough for you, Chapters 4 and 8 can set you straight.)

Selecting Prepositions

Prepositions are words that go in front of nouns and show a relationship in time or space (*under* the counter, *over* the top). Of all the tens of thousands of words in the English language, fewer than 200 of them are prepositions. And yet, three of those little words make it into the Top Ten Most Used Words in English (no, not 'I love you'— none of those words are prepositions). Those three little words are — *of, in* and *to.*

No rules really exist about how to choose the right preposition — you're just supposed to know which one goes where — by language osmosis. Your dictionary is the place to find the help you may need. Look carefully at prepositions when you're editing your work. They can be very troublesome.

Here are a few examples so that you know what you're looking for

> This sentence has an extra preposition (shown with the strikethrough): *Tom's sunglasses fell off ~~of~~ the dashboard.*

This sentence contains the wrong preposition (with the correct one shown in round brackets): *I'm bored ~~of~~ (with) this.*

So does this one: *She's angry ~~at~~ (with) me.* And this one is missing the preposition *on*: *They went to the movie (on) Sunday afternoon.*

And here are a few solutions to common preposition problems that tend to trip people up:

- In Australia, it is best to use *different from* — not *different than* or *different to.*

- *Beside* means positioned next to. *Besides* means as well, or moreover. It is a joining word, not a preposition.

- In general, *between* is used when you're taking about two things. *Among* is used for larger groups.

- You do something either *on* purpose or *by* accident.

Confusing 'Of' with 'Have'

Aussies are famous for effortlessly turning most vowel sounds into a multi-purpose grunt. When we abbreviate *would have* to *would've*, the word that comes out of our mouths sounds like *would of*. So that's what people write. Solution: Don't do it!

Index

Notes

Want to learn more about English grammar?

In the book, you'll find:

- Help with refining your style

- Details about the different levels of English, including 'friendspeak' and 'txtspk'

- How to achieve accuracy in electronic communication — eGrammar

- Ways to edit and proofread your writing